DASH DIET COOKBOOK
THE LOW SODIUM RECIPES TO LOWER YOUR BLOOD PRESSURE AND REDUCE THE RISK OF MANY CHRONIC CONDITIONS WITH 4-WEEK EASY-TO FOLLOW MEAL PLAN

Table of Contents

Introduction 8
Chapter 1.   What to eat and what to avoid 9
    Dash diet for weight loss 9
    Dash diet for health 9
    Forbidden foods 9
    Recommended foods 9
    Dash diet food list 10
Chapter 2.   4-week Meal Plan 11
    First Week 11
    Second Week 11
    Third Week 12
    Fourth Week 12
Chapter 3.   Breakfast 13
    1.   *Antioxidant Smoothie Bowl* 13
    2.   *Fragrant Shakshuka* 13
    3.   *Avo Trout Toastie* 14
    4.   *Veg Breakfast Taco* 14
    5.   *Colorful Citrus Smoothie* 14
    6.   *Raspberry Polenta Waffles* 15
    7.   *Stone Fruit Quinoa* 15
    8.   *Fruity Breakfast Muffins* 16
    9.   *Mushroom Frittata* 16
    10. *Sweet Potato and Bean Fry Up* 17
    11. *Bacon Bits* 17
    12. *Steel Cut Oat Blueberry Pancakes* 17
    13. *Spinach, Mushroom, and Feta Cheese Scramble* 18
    14. *Red Velvet Pancakes with Cream Cheese Topping* 18
    15. *Peanut Butter and Banana Breakfast Smoothie* 18
    16. *No-Bake Breakfast Granola Bars* 19
    17. *Mushroom Shallot Frittata* 19
    18. *Jack-o-Lantern Pancakes* 20
    19. *Fruit Pizza* 20
    20. *Flax Banana Yogurt Muffins* 20
    21. *Apple Oats* 21
    22. *Buckwheat Crepes* 21
    23. *Whole Grain Pancakes* 21
    24. *Granola Parfait* 22
    25. *Curry Tofu Scramble* 22
    26. *Easy Veggie Muffins* 22
    27. *Carrot Muffins* 23
    28. *Pineapple Oatmeal* 23
    29. *Spinach Muffins* 23
    30. *Chia Seeds Breakfast Mix* 24
    31. *Breakfast Fruits Bowls* 24
    32. *Pumpkin Cookies* 24
    33. *Veggie Scramble* 24
    34. *Mushrooms and Turkey Breakfast* 25
    35. *Mushrooms and Cheese Omelet* 25
Chapter 4.   Lunch 26
    36. *Gnocchi with Tomato Basil Sauce* 26
    37. *Creamy Pumpkin Pasta* 26

38.	Mexican-Style Potato Casserole	27
39.	Black Bean Stew with Cornbread	27
40.	Mushroom Florentine	28
41.	Hassel back Eggplant	28
42.	Vegetarian Kebabs	29
43.	White Beans Stew	29
44.	Vegetarian Lasagna	29
45.	Pan-Fried Salmon with Salad	30
46.	Veggie Variety	30
47.	Vegetable Pasta	30
48.	Vegetable Noodles with Bolognese	31
49.	Black Bean Burgers with Lettuce "Buns"	31
50.	Curry Vegetable Noodles with Chicken	32
51.	Tempeh Veggie Tacos	32
52.	Chickpea Frittata with Tomatoes and Watercress	33
53.	Harissa Bolognese with Vegetable Noodles	33
54.	Roasted Apple–Butternut Squash Soup	34
55.	Sweet and Sour Vegetable Noodles	34
56.	Tuna Sandwich	35
57.	Sweet Potatoes and Zucchini Soup	35
58.	Lemongrass and Chicken Soup	35
59.	Easy Lunch Salmon Steaks	36
60.	Light Balsamic Salad	36
61.	Purple Potato Soup	36
62.	Leeks Soup	37
63.	Cauliflower Lunch Salad	37
64.	Tofu and Green Bean Stir Fry	37
65.	Spicy Tofu Burrito Bowls with Cilantro Avocado Sauce	38
66.	Chickpea Cauliflower Tikka Masala	39
67.	Eggplant Parmesan Stacks	39
68.	Tomato and Olive Orecchiette with Basil Pesto	40
69.	Italian Stuffed Portobello Mushroom Burgers	40
70.	French Toast Sticks with Yogurt-Berry Dipping Sauce	40
Chapter 5.	**Dinner**	**42**
71.	Apple Pie Crackers	42
72.	Orange and Chili Garlic Sauce	42
73.	Tantalizing Mushroom Gravy	42
74.	Everyday Vegetable Stock	43
75.	Grilled Chicken with Lemon and Fennel	43
76.	Black Eyed Peas and Spinach Platter	44
77.	Humble Mushroom Rice	44
78.	Roasted Root Vegetables with Goat's Cheese Polenta	44
79.	Fish Stew	45
80.	Gnocchi Pomodoro	45
81.	Slow-Cooked Pasta e Fagioli Soup	46
82.	Salmon Couscous Salad	46
83.	Roasted Salmon with Smoky Chickpeas and Greens	47
84.	Salmon with Salsa	47
85.	Bruschetta Chicken	48
86.	Quinoa Power Salad	48
87.	Balsamic Roast Chicken Breast	49
88.	Stuffed Eggplant Shells	49
89.	Zucchini Pepper Kebabs	50

90.	Corn Stuffed Peppers	50
91.	South Asian Baked salmon	51
92.	Sweet Potato Carbonara with Spinach and Mushrooms	51
93.	Hazelnut-Parsley Roast Tilapia	52
94.	Fig and Goat's Cheese Salad	52
95.	Masala Chickpeas	53
96.	Orecchiette with Broccoli Rabe	53
97.	Chicken and Strawberry Salad	54
98.	Mixed Vegetable Salad with Lime Dressing	54
99.	Spinach Ginger Lentils	55
100.	Basil Halibut	55
101.	Leek and Cauliflower Soup	55
102.	Sweet and Sour Cabbage and Apples	56
103.	Delicious Aloo Palak	56
104.	Hasselback Eggplant Parmesan	57
105.	Chicken Caesar Pasta Salad	57

Chapter 6. Snack 59

106.	Pumpkin Pie Fat Bombs	59
107.	Sweet Almond and Coconut Fat Bombs	59
108.	Apricot Biscotti	59
109.	Apple and Berry Cobbler	60
110.	Mixed Fruit Compote Cups	60
111.	Generous Garlic Bread Stick	61
112.	Cauliflower Bread Stick	61
113.	Cocktail Wieners	62
114.	Pressure Cooker Braised Pulled Ham	62
115.	Mini Teriyaki Turkey Sandwiches	62
116.	Peach Crumble Muffins	63
117.	Cranberry Hot Wings	63
118.	Almond and Tomato Balls	64
119.	Avocado Tuna Bites	64
120.	Hearty Buttery Walnuts	64
121.	Refreshing Watermelon Sorbet	65
122.	Faux Mac and Cheese	65
123.	Banana Custard	65
124.	Healthy Tahini Buns	66
125.	Sautéed Swiss Chard	66
126.	Asian Style Asparagus	66
127.	Aromatic Cauliflower Florets	67
128.	Brussel Sprouts Mix	67
129.	Braised Baby Carrot	67
130.	Acorn Squash with Apples	68
131.	Asparagus with Horseradish Dip	68
132.	Grilled Tomatoes	68
133.	Parsley Celery Root	69
134.	Garlic Black Eyed Peas	69
135.	Braised Artichokes	69
136.	Grilled Eggplant Slices	70
137.	Lentil Sauté	70
138.	Italian Style Zucchini Coins	70
139.	Brussels sprouts with Shallots and Lemon	71
140.	Chili-Lime Grilled Pineapple	71

Chapter 7. Veggies 72

141.	Zucchini Fritters with Corn Salsa	72
142.	Zucchini Lasagna Roll-Ups	72
143.	Toasted Chickpea-Quinoa Bowl	73
144.	Fried Pasta Chips with Tomato-Basil Dip	73
145.	Penne with Sizzling Tomatoes and Artichokes	74
146.	Black Bean Bake with Avocado	75
147.	Falafel with Mint-Tahini Sauce	75
148.	Quinoa-Lentil Burgers	76
149.	Eggplant Bites with Marinara	76
150.	Broccoli Salad	77
151.	Kale, Quinoa, and Avocado Salad	77
152.	Garden Salad	78
153.	Baked Smoky Broccoli and Garlic	78
154.	Roasted Cauliflower and Lima Beans	79
155.	Cauliflower Salad with Tahini Vinaigrette	79
156.	White Beans with Spinach and Pan-Roasted Tomatoes	80
157.	Bean Hummus	80
158.	Hasselback Eggplant	80
159.	Black-Eyed Peas and Greens Power Salad	81
160.	Butternut-Squash Macaroni and Cheese	81
161.	Healthy Vegetable Fried Rice	81
162.	Carrot Cakes	82
163.	Vegan Chili	82
164.	Aromatic Whole Grain Spaghetti	82
165.	Chunky Tomatoes	83
166.	Baby minted carrots	83
167.	Baked Falafel	83
168.	Paella	84
169.	Mushroom Cakes	84
170.	Glazed Eggplant Rings	85
171.	Sweet Potato Balls	85
172.	Chickpea Curry	85
173.	Quinoa Bowl	86
174.	Vegan Meatloaf	86
175.	Loaded Potato Skins	86
Chapter 8.	**Desserts**	**88**
176.	Banana-Cashew Cream Mousse	88
177.	Cherry Stew	88
178.	Sriracha Parsnip Fries	88
179.	Tortilla Strawberry Chips	89
180.	Almond Rice Pudding	89
181.	Sweet Potatoes and Apples Mix	89
182.	Sautéed Bananas with Orange Sauce	90
183.	Caramelized Blood Oranges with Ginger Cream	90
184.	Grilled Minted Watermelon	91
185.	Caramelized Apricot Pots	91
186.	Pumpkin Pie	91
187.	Chocolate Avocado Mousse	92
188.	Lemon Cheesecake	92
189.	Apple and Almond Muffins	92
190.	Toasted Almond Ambrosia	93
191.	Key Lime Cherry "Nice" Cream	93
192.	Tart Raspberry Crumble Bar	94

193.	Easy Coconut-Carrot Cake Balls	94
194.	Apple Dumplings	95
195.	Cauliflower Cinnamon Pudding	95
196.	Coconut Mousse	95
197.	Mango Pudding	96
198.	Rhubarb Pie	96
199.	Fruit Skewers	97
200.	Pumpkin Pudding	97
201.	Pop Corn Bites	97
202.	Delicious Berry Pie	97
203.	Gentle Sweet Potato Tempura	98
204.	Delightful Pizza Dip	98
205.	Strawberry Cheesecake	99
206.	Strawberries and Cream Cheese Crepes	99
207.	Apple-Berry Cobbler	99
208.	Vanilla Poached Peaches	100
209.	Mixed Berry Whole-Grain Cake	100
210.	Ambrosia with Coconut and Toasted Almonds	101

Chapter 9. Index 102
Chapter 10. BONUS: VIDEO LECTURES 105
Conclusion 106

Introduction

The dash diet is an eating plan proven to help people lose weight, lower their blood pressure, and reduce the risk of many chronic conditions. A dash diet cookbook is a must-have for anyone who wants to get the most out of this healthy, easy-to-follow eating plan. Your body needs the proper nutrients to stay healthy, so you should eat the right foods from all the different food groups on a dash diet plan. The dash diet is one of several that all work in the same way: they provide a list of foods that are free to eat and foods that should be avoided to lose weight. The dash diet is related to the low-carb diet but restricts fat, sodium, and calories.

The dash diet is a collection of eating plans that take their cue from the (DASH) Dietary Approaches to Stop Hypertension eating guide developed by the U.S. The U.S. government has given a seal of approval to the dash diet as an eating plan that is simple to execute and will let people attain their goals of eating healthy foods that are low in fat. A dash diet cookbook is one of the best ways to get set up on this eating plan and learn how to make healthy meals that taste great. When you follow a diet, you have guidance on what foods you can eat and what you should avoid. A dash diet cookbook will let you start this healthy eating plan immediately.

To keep the dash diet healthy, you should follow the rules of eating healthy foods. On a dash diet, you should eat vegetables, fruits, fish, poultry, and whole grains. These foods are high in vitamins and low in fat and minerals that your body needs to stay healthy. Some foods you want to eat less or avoid altogether on a dash diet include red meat, sweets, and high-fat dairy products.

If you do not have enough time to make healthy meals, a dash diet cookbook may answer your problem. The dash diet is tailored toward people without much time to spend in the kitchen. This will help you eat healthily without changing your hectic lifestyle. You can still eat great meals that are low in fat and high in vitamins and minerals.

Many families are losing time in their busy schedules, which has led them to other unhealthy eating habits that may lead to health problems. The dash diet was developed to help families find the time to eat healthy foods while keeping busy schedules. Cooking healthy nutrition will help you and your family maintain a healthy lifestyle and avoid health problems linked to unhealthy eating. You can devour nutritious meals by using recipes with flavor and taste in every bite. With the help of a dash diet cookbook, you can get your family to eat healthier without feeling like they are missing out.

Chapter 1. What to eat and what to avoid

Dash diet is not so much a specific recipe; it is a cooking process that uses less or no salt while maintaining the same flavor. It uses one-quarter teaspoon or less salt per serving. The Dash diet was designed for people at risk of high blood pressure or already suffering from it. The higher your blood pressure, the more significant your risk for heart disease, stroke, and kidney disease. Salt is a critical component in high blood pressure and its health risks. By reducing salt intake, a person reduces the risk for these illnesses. Another benefit of the Dash diet is that it is pretty easy to follow. The ingredients are not hard to find, despite some people thinking they are hard to come by in their area.

Dash diet for weight loss

The Dash diet is a precise way to lose weight, but it's also very healthy. You can eat delicious food without salt and still have incredible health benefits. The average person will not have to change their cooking or eating habits to follow the Dash diet successfully. It is also feasible to combine the Dash diet with many other diets. Whether you are vegetarian or vegan, you can still follow this plan because of the variety provided through some recipes. It can be challenging to follow the Dash diet without being well-informed and without guidance. For one thing, it's hard to know exactly how much salt you are using in a recipe when you don't measure it. Many people also become frustrated when they find that they're following all of their recipes perfectly and aren't losing weight. The solution is to incorporate the Dash diet into your life as much as possible. A simple way to do this is by taking daily measurements of the salt you use in a recipe. If you turn down on salt, you will find that some recipes no longer call for as much and that others only need a little more. Taking measurements also makes it easier to start the Dash diet because you will have a better idea of how much food will be enough for your body when you cut down on salt.

Dash diet for health

The Dash diet can also be very healthy because it allows you to choose foods that are better for you. Many ingredients are naturally low in sodium because sodium can harm your heart and lead to high blood pressure. The Dash diet uses more vegetables than other diets because they have less sodium. Plenty of recipes will work very well with fewer amounts of salt, and you will find that they taste just as good. The flexibility in the diet also makes it possible for you to choose foods that are good for you. People with high blood pressure or a diet high in sodium often have trouble making healthy food options because they don't know what is healthy. When people know that a portion of food is unhealthy, they tend to make healthier choices about what to eat so their health won't be at risk. Even though the Dash diet is a great way to lose weight, it is also very healthy. You can eat delicious food with little or no salt, and you will still improve your health. The truth is you can eat delicious foods that contain less salt and still get the same health benefits makes this diet very flexible and easy to follow.

Forbidden foods

- All condiments, sauces and gravies
- Pickles-Snack foods, chips, crackers, and popcorn
- All packaged foods with artificial flavorings or seasoned salts
- Soups and broths with added salt

On the other hand:

The USDA recommends daily consumption of 2300 mg of sodium. The DASH diet limits this to 1,500 mg per day. Individuals can significantly reduce their salt intake by reducing the amount of salt used in cooking. The average amount of sodium consumed in the US is 50-60 grams daily, equivalent to about three cups of salt.

Recommended foods

- Vegetables: all vegetables are encouraged; 2 1/2 cups of vegetables are recommended for each meal.
- Fresh fruits: unlimited consumption; 2 cups are recommended.
- Whole grains: 6 servings of whole grains per day; three should be bread.

- Low-fat or nonfat dairy products: 3 to 4 servings of low-fat milk and milk products per day.
- Protein foods: fish and shellfish, lean meats and poultry without skin; nuts and legumes; eggs; beans.

Dash diet food list

- Grains: Loaves of bread, Pasta, Rice: Grains are eaten unlimitedly and will account for most of the day's calories. Most grains should be whole grains. Whole grain bread has all the same nutrients as refined grain bread but retains more fiber, which is good for you. Eat whole-grain cereal or oatmeal instead of refined grains.
- Fruits are eaten as snacks throughout the day and in unlimited quantities. 2 cups of fruit are recommended for each meal. Eat fresh fruits in abundance.
- Vegetables: Vegetables are eaten for every meal, but it is recommended that a person eat 6 or more servings per day; three should be salads. Eat all vegetables, raw or cooked.
- Protein: 4 to 6 ounces of lean meat (including poultry), fish, and shellfish daily. Meat and poultry are the best protein sources for health, which is why the DASH diet encourages many of these foods.
- Fat-free or low-fat dairy: 3 or more servings of fat-free milk and 2 or more servings of fat-free yogurt daily

The typical American diet is full of salt and sodium, which is a major contributing factor to high blood pressure in many cases. People who are often on the go may have difficulty following this diet due to their hectic lifestyles. Being on the go doesn't mean you can't eat well. Eating a lot at home makes it easy to reduce your salt intake. The DASH diet is not only for people who have hypertension or high blood pressure. It is also for people who want to eat a healthier diet. Low salt diets are recommended for anyone with high blood pressure; however, following this diet will also deal with other health benefits, such as lowering your heart disease and stroke risk.

Chapter 2. 4-week Meal Plan

First Week

DAY	BREAKFAST	LUNCH	DINNER	SNACK
Day-1	Antioxidant Smoothie Bowl	Gnocchi with Tomato Basil Sauce	Apple Pie Crackers	Pumpkin Pie Fat Bombs
Day-2	Fragrant Shakshuka	Creamy Pumpkin Pasta	Orange and Chili Garlic Sauce	Sweet Almond and Coconut Fat Bombs
Day-3	Avo Trout Toastie	Mexican-Style Potato Casserole	Tantalizing Mushroom Gravy	Apricot Biscotti
Day4	Veg Breakfast Taco	Black Bean Stew with Cornbread	Everyday Vegetable Stock	Apple and Berry Cobbler
Day-5	Colorful Citrus Smoothie	Mushroom Florentine	Grilled Chicken with Lemon and Fennel	Mixed Fruit Compote Cups
Day-6	Raspberry Polenta Waffles	Hassel back Eggplant	Black Eyed Peas and Spinach Platter	Generous Garlic Bread Stick
Day-7	Stone Fruit Quinoa	Vegetarian Kebabs	Humble Mushroom Rice	Cauliflower Bread Stick

Second Week

DAY	BREAKFAST	LUNCH	DINNER	SNACK
Day-1	Fruity Breakfast Muffins	White Beans Stew	Roasted Root Vegetables With Goat's Cheese Polenta	Cocktail Wieners
Day-2	Mushroom Frittata	Vegetarian Lasagna	Fish Stew	Pressure Cooker Braised Pulled Ham
Day-3	Sweet Potato and Bean Fry Up	Pan-Fried Salmon with Salad	Gnocchi Pomodoro	Mini Teriyaki Turkey Sandwiches
Day4	Bacon Bits	Veggie Variety	Slow-Cooked Pasta e Fagioli Soup	Peach Crumble Muffins
Day-5	Steel Cut Oat Blueberry Pancakes	Vegetable Pasta	Salmon Couscous Salad	Cranberry Hot Wings
Day-6	Spinach, Mushroom, and Feta Cheese Scramble	Vegetable Noodles with Bolognese	Roasted Salmon with Smoky Chickpeas and Greens	Almond and Tomato Balls
Day-7	Red Velvet Pancakes with Cream Cheese Topping	Black Bean Burgers with Lettuce "Buns"	Salmon with Salsa	Avocado Tuna Bites

Third Week

DAY	BREAKFAST	LUNCH	DINNER	SNACK
Day-1	Peanut Butter and Banana Breakfast Smoothie	Curry Vegetable Noodles with Chicken	Bruschetta Chicken	Hearty Buttery Walnuts
Day-2	No-Bake Breakfast Granola Bars	Tempeh Veggie Tacos	Quinoa Power Salad	Refreshing Watermelon Sorbet
Day-3	Mushroom Shallot Frittata	Chickpea Frittata with Tomatoes and Watercress	Balsamic Roast Chicken Breast	Faux Mac and Cheese
Day4	Jack-o-Lantern Pancakes	Harissa Bolognese with Vegetable Noodles	Stuffed Eggplant Shells	Banana Custard
Day-5	Fruit Pizza	Roasted Apple–Butternut Squash Soup	Zucchini Pepper Kebabs	Healthy Tahini Buns
Day-6	Flax Banana Yogurt Muffins	Sweet and Sour Vegetable Noodles	Corn Stuffed Peppers	Sautéed Swiss Chard
Day-7	Apple Oats	Tuna Sandwich	South Asian Baked salmon	Asian Style Asparagus

Fourth Week

DAY	BREAKFAST	LUNCH	DINNER	SNACK
Day-1	Buckwheat Crepes	Sweet Potatoes and Zucchini Soup	Sweet Potato Carbonara with Spinach and Mushrooms	Aromatic Cauliflower Florets
Day-2	Whole Grain Pancakes	Lemongrass and Chicken Soup	Hazelnut-Parsley Roast Tilapia	Brussel Sprouts Mix
Day-3	Granola Parfait	Easy Lunch Salmon Steaks	Fig and Goat's Cheese Salad	Braised Baby Carrot
Day4	Curry Tofu Scramble	Light Balsamic Salad	Masala Chickpeas	Acorn Squash with Apples
Day-5	Easy Veggie Muffins	Purple Potato Soup	Orecchiette with Broccoli Rabe	Asparagus with Horseradish Dip
Day-6	Carrot Muffins	Leeks Soup	Chicken and Strawberry Salad	Grilled Tomatoes
Day-7	Pineapple Oatmeal	Cauliflower Lunch Salad	Mixed Vegetable Salad with Lime Dressing	Parsley Celery Root

Chapter 3. Breakfast

1. Antioxidant Smoothie Bowl

Preparation time: 17 minutes Cooking time: 0 Servings: 1
Ingredients:
Smoothie:
- 2 tbsp. chia gel (see step 1)
- 1/2 medium frozen banana, cut into pieces
- 3/4 cup cherries, frozen
- 1/2 cup coconut yogurt
- 1 tbsp. pure cocoa powder
- 1 tbsp. macadamia nut butter
- 1 cup fresh chard
- 1 teaspoon vanilla extract
- 1/2 cup unsweetened nut milk.
- 3-4 ice cubes

To serve:
- 1/2 tbsp. cocoa nibs
- Fresh berries
- Toasted macadamia nuts, roughly chopped
- 1/2 banana thinly sliced
- Dried goji berries

Directions:
1. Make your chia gel first – Mix 1/3cup chia seeds and 2 cups water well. A nice way to do this is to combine the ingredients in a jar and shake it for about 15 seconds. Let the gel rest for 1 minute, then shake/mix again and put it into the fridge for about 10 minutes until it forms a firm gel.
2. Then blend all the smoothie ingredients on high in a blender until you have a beautifully smooth, creamy smoothie. Ensure not to make it too runny by adding the milk little by little
3. Serve topped with the toppings of your choice arranged beautifully, with a sprinkle of cocoa powder to finish.

Nutrition:
Calories: 412 Protein: 20g Fat: 14g
Carbs: 7g Sodium: 28mg Potassium: 120mg

2. Fragrant Shakshuka

Preparation time: 10 minutes Cooking time: 40 minutes Servings: 4
Ingredients:
- 1 shallot, diced
- 2 cloves of garlic, finely chopped
- 2 fresh paprika peppers, deseeded and diced
- 1/2 tsp. dried smoked paprika
- 1/2 tsp. dried ground cumin
- 1 tbsp. olive oil
- 28-ounce jar/tin pre-made, low sodium marinara sauce
- 1 cup fresh chard, chopped
- 8 eggs
- 1/4 low fat feta cheese
- 1 avocado
- Fresh coriander, finely chopped, to serve
- 2 small focaccia breads, toasted and cut into 8 pieces

Directions:
1. Gently fry the shallot, garlic, and fresh paprika in the oil until the shallots are soft.
2. Add the dry spices, and after 1 minute, add your marinara sauce. Gently cook the sauce for approximately 20 min until nicely reduced and flavorful.
3. Add the chard and stir in.
4. Before the chard has time to overcook, make 8 indents in your sauce, using the back of a large spoon. Crack the eggs into each of these indents. Cover the pan with a lid and gently poach the eggs in the sauce for about 6-8 minutes, until the whites are firm and the yolks are done to perfection.

5. Serve with toasted focaccia, crumbled feta, coriander, and sliced avocado. Enjoy hot off the stove!

Nutrition:

Calories: 454	Protein: 18g	Fat: 29g
Carbs: 4.5g	Sodium: 104mg	Potassium: 220mg

3. Avo Trout Toastie

Preparation time: 5 minutes   Cooking time: 3 minutes   Servings: 2

Ingredients:
- 2 Sesame bagels, cut in half
- 1 big avocado
- 3 ounces cold smoked rainbow trout
- Freshly squeezed lemon juice
- Freshly ground black pepper
- Fresh parsley, shredded
- 2 black cherry tomatoes, cut into slices

Directions:
1. Gently toast the bagels under the grill or in a flat pan on a very low heat.
2. While the bagels toast, cut, peel, and pit the avocados, then place in a bowl with a tablespoon of lemon juice, and smash lightly.
3. To serve: smear the avocado evenly over the bagel halves. Lay the tomato slices down, and top with the smoked trout.
4. Set it off with a generous splash of lemon juice over the fish and some freshly ground black pepper and fresh parsley to taste.

Nutrition:

Calories: 382	Protein: 19g	Fat: 20g
Carbs: 3g	Sodium: 90mg	Potassium: 380 mg

4. Veg Breakfast Taco

Preparation time: 5 minutes   Cooking time: 7 minutes   Servings: 2

Ingredients:
- 3 large eggs
- 1/4 cup low fat milk
- 1 tbsp. olive oil
- 3 small yellow, red, and green bell peppers, diced
- 1 shallot finely chopped
- 2 cups baby spinach, fresh
- 1/2 tsp. paprika
- Black pepper to taste
- 2 tbsp. crumbled feta cheese
- 2 soft-shell tacos

Directions:
1. Whisk together the eggs, milk, paprika, and pepper in a bowl, and set aside.
2. Warmth the oil in a pan, then attach the shallot and peppers and cook on low heat for about 3 minutes. The onion will go soft and translucent. Attach the baby spinach, turn off the heat, and cover with a lid. Allow spinach to wilt for about 2 minutes.
3. Turn the heat back on and add the egg mixture. Gently stir the eggs until cooked. (About 2 minutes).
4. Serve spooned into the soft-shell tacos and topped with feta cheese.

Nutrition:

Calories: 397	Protein: 16g	Fat: 30g
Carbs: 5g	Sodium: 50mg	Potassium: 320 mg

5. Colorful Citrus Smoothie

Preparation time: 5 minutes   Cooking time: 0 minutes   Servings: 1

Ingredients:
- 1/2 cup cooked, sliced beetroot
- 1/2 cup frozen blueberries
- 1/2 of 1 Cara Cara orange, peeled and frozen

- 3/4 cup unsweetened oat milk
- 1 tbsp. hemp seeds
- 1 tsp. honey
- 3 olives
- 1/2 tsp. vanilla essence
- 1/2 cup low fat Greek yogurt
- 3-4 ice cubes
- 1/2 tsp. guar- and/or xanthan gum

Directions:
1. Blend the oat milk and hemp seeds together on low for 20-30 seconds.
2. Attach the remaining ingredients and blend on high until thick, smooth and creamy.

Nutrition:
Calories: 251　　Protein: 17g　　Fat: 6g
Carbs: 2g　　Sodium: 139mg　　Potassium: 220mg

6. Raspberry Polenta Waffles

Preparation time: 15 minutes　　Cooking time: 20 minutes　　Servings: 8

Ingredients:
- 1 tbsp. unsalted butter, melted
- 1 tbsp. sunflower oil
- 1 1/4 cups low fat milk
- 1 cup plain cake flour
- 2 tbsp. caster sugar
- 1 cup finely ground polenta
- 1 1/2 tsp. baking powder
- 2 large egg whites
- 2 cups low fat, plain yogurt
- 6 ounces raspberries, for serving
- Sunflower oil in a spray bottle for the waffle iron

Directions:
1. Mix the milk, oil, and melted butter together in a bowl.
2. Sift the flour, sugar, polenta, and baking powder into a separate bowl, whisk gently, then stir in the milk mixture until just combined. Set aside.
3. Set the oven to 200°F to preheat and turn on your waffle iron to warm up.
4. In an electric mixer, set the egg whites until stiff peaks form. Gently fold 2/3 of the egg whites into the flour mixture, add the last 1/3 and fold in.
5. Oil the waffle iron lightly, and then add about 1 cup of the waffle batter into the iron. Close and let cook until they are golden brown and cooked through.
6. To serve, place 2 waffles on a plate stacked on top of each other. Spoon 1/4 cup yogurt over them and cascade a handful of raspberries over the top.
7. Enjoy warm!

Nutrition:
Calories: 233　　Fiber: 2g　　Potassium: 150mg
Carbs: 8g　　Sodium: 119mg
Protein: 9g　　Fat: 5g

7. Stone Fruit Quinoa

Preparation time: 5 minutes　　Cooking time: 20 minutes　　Servings: 4

Ingredients:
- 1 cup finely chopped fresh apricots
- 1/2 tsp. ground cinnamon
- 2 cups low fat milk
- 1 cup quinoa, rinsed and drained
- 2 tbsp. chopped pecan nuts
- 2 tbsp. honey

Directions:
1. Place the apricots, cinnamon, milk, and quinoa in a medium pot, and bring to a boil.
2. Set the heat to low and cook for about 20 minutes. The quinoa will absorb most of the liquid by this stage.
3. Set off the heat and let stand with the lid on for about 5 minutes.
4. Using a fork, incorporate air into the quinoa by whisking gently.

5. Serve hot, with pecans sprinkled over it and a drizzle of honey to sweeten.

Nutrition:

Calories: 245 — Protein: 11g — Fat: 5g
Carbs: 4.1g — Sodium: 81mg — Potassium: 198mg

8. Fruity Breakfast Muffins

Preparation time: 15 minutes — Cooking time: 22 minutes — Servings: 6

Ingredients:
- 1 cup cake flour
- 1/2 cup rolled oats
- 1 tsp. baking powder
- 1/2 tsp. mixed spice
- 2 ripe bananas
- 1/3 cup castor sugar
- 1/2 tsp. vanilla essence
- 1/4 cup sunflower oil
- 1 egg
- Spay and cook
- 1 cup fresh cranberries

Directions:
1. Set the oven on to 350F to preheat it.
2. Set together the cake flour, baking powder, and mixed spice in a bowl. Then add the oats.
3. In other bowl, mash up the bananas, then add the caster sugar. Mix well, then add the vanilla, oil, and egg and whisk to combine.
4. Mix the dry and wet ingredients in a bowl, then add the cranberries.
5. Spray a 6-cup muffin tray with Spray and Cook, then divide the mixture evenly amongst the muffin cups.
6. Bake for about 20-22 minutes, or until, when a skewer is inserted into the middle, it comes out clean.

Nutrition:

Calories: 305 — Protein: 7g — Fat: 11g
Carbs: 4.7g — Sodium: 66mg — Potassium: 156mg

9. Mushroom Frittata

Preparation time: 10 minutes — Cooking time: 10 minutes — Servings: 2

Ingredients:
- 1 tsp. unsalted butter, melted
- Spray and Cook
- 1 large brown mushroom, sliced
- 1/2 cup chopped oyster mushroom
- 2 tbsp. minced onion
- 3 large eggs
- 1/2 cup sour cream
- Black pepper to taste
- Cherry tomatoes to serve
- 1 sprig basil to serve

Directions:
1. Spray a medium non-stick pan with Spray and Cook to prevent any sticking.
2. Add the butter to the pan and fry up the onion and mushrooms gently for 3-4 minutes.
3. Set together the eggs and sour cream until well combined. Add black pepper to taste.
4. Turn on the grill function on your oven and allow to heat.
5. Attach the egg mixture to the pan and cook gently on low for 2 minutes.
6. Set the pan under the grill for about 1-2 minutes until the top of your frittata is a beautiful golden color.
7. To serve, untighten the edges of the frittata using a spatula. Place a large plate over the top of the pan and then invert it, allowing the frittata to turn over onto the plate.
8. Scatter cherry tomatoes over the top of the frittata and place the basil in the center. Cut and serve warm.

Nutrition:

Calories: 232 — Protein: 18g — Fat: 15g
Carbs: 7g — Sodium: 129mg — Potassium: 240mg

10. Sweet Potato and Bean Fry Up

Preparation time: 10 minutes   Cooking time: 10 minutes   Servings: 3

Ingredients:
- 1 cup sweet potato, washed and diced
- 1 tbsp. olive oil
- 1 tsp. ground paprika
- 1 can of red kidney beans- 15 ounces
- 1 cup rice zucchini*
- 2 cups baby spinach finely chopped
- 4 cherry tomatoes halved
- Black pepper to taste
- 1-ounce roasted pumpkin seeds, unsalted
- 1/4 cup fresh coriander, chopped

Directions:
1. In a medium-sized pan with high sides, heat the olive oil until a piece of sweet potato placed in the pan sizzles. Add the sweet potato and fry on medium heat for about 5 minutes until browned and cooked through.
2. Then add in the riced zucchini, red kidney beans, paprika, and cherry tomatoes. Cook for about 4 minutes until all the ingredients have heated through. Then add the baby spinach, and wilt for 1 minute. Add black pepper to taste.
3. Serve hot, topped with toasted seeds and chopped herbs.

Nutrition:
Calories: 298   Protein: 14g   Fat: 10g
Carbs: 4.2g   Sodium: 45mg   Potassium: 179mg

11. Bacon Bits

Preparation time: 15 minutes   Cooking time: 60 minutes   Servings: 4

Ingredients:
- 1 cup Millet
- 5 cup water
- 1 cup sweet potato, diced
- 1 tsp. cinnamon, ground
- 2 tbsp. brown sugar
- 1 medium apple, diced
- 1/4 cup honey

Directions:
1. In a deep pot, attach your sugar, sweet potato, cinnamon, water, and millet, then stir to merge, then boil on high heat. After that, simmer on low.
2. Cook like this for about an hour, until your water is fully absorbed and millet is cooked. Stir in your remaining ingredients and serve.

Nutrition:
Calories: 136   Protein: 3.1 g   Sodium: 120 mg
Carbs: 2.5 g   Fat: 1.0 g   Potassium: 120mg

12. Steel Cut Oat Blueberry Pancakes

Preparation time: 15 minutes   Cooking time: 15 minutes   Servings: 4

Ingredients:
- 1 1/2 cup water
- 1/2 cup steel-cut oats
- 1/4 tsp. salt
- 1 cup whole-wheat flour
- 1/2 tsp. baking powder
- 1/2 tsp. baking soda
- 1 egg
- 1 cup milk
- 1/2 cup Greek yogurt
- 1 cup blueberries, frozen
- 3/4 cup agave nectar

Directions:
1. Combine your oats, salt, and water in a medium saucepan, stir, and allow to come to a boil over high heat. Adjust the heat to low, and allow to simmer for about 10 min, or until oats get tender. Set aside.

2. Merge all your remaining ingredients, except agave nectar, in a medium bowl, then fold in oats. Preheat your skillet, and lightly grease it. Cook 1/4 cup of milk batter at a time for about 3 minutes per side. Garnish with Agave Nectar.

Nutrition:
Calories: 257
Carbs: 4.6 g
Protein: 14 g
Fat: 7 g
Sodium: 123 mg
Potassium: 130mg

13. Spinach, Mushroom, and Feta Cheese Scramble

Preparation time: 15 minutes
Cooking time: 4 minutes
Servings: 1

Ingredients:
- Olive oil cooking spray
- 1/2 cup mushroom, sliced
- 1 cup spinach, chopped
- 3 eggs
- 2 tbsp. Feta cheese
- Pepper

Directions:
1. Set a lightly greased, medium skillet over medium heat. Attach spinach and mushrooms, and cook until spinach wilts.
2. Merge egg whites, cheese, pepper, and whole egg in a medium bowl, whisk to combine. Spill into your skillet and cook, while stirring, until set for 4 minutes.
3. Serve.

Nutrition:
Calories: 236.5
Carbs: 12.9 g
Protein: 22.2 g
Fat: 11. 4g
Sodium: 105 mg
Potassium: 120mg

14. Red Velvet Pancakes with Cream Cheese Topping

Preparation time: 15 minutes
Cooking time: 10 minutes
Servings: 2

Ingredients:
Cream Cheese Topping:
- 2 oz. cream cheese
- 3 tbsp. yogurt
- 3 tbsp. honey
- 1 tbsp. milk

Pancakes:
- 1/2 cup whole wheat flour
- 1/2 cup all-purpose flour
- 2 1/4 tsps. baking powder
- 1/2 tsp. cocoa powder, unsweetened
- 1/4 tsp. salt
- 1/4 cup sugar
- 1 large egg
- 1 cup + 2 tbsp. Milk
- 1 tsp. vanilla
- 1 tsp. red paste food coloring

Directions:
1. Merge all your topping ingredients in a medium bowl, and set aside. Add all your pancake ingredients to a large bowl and fold until combined. Set a greased skillet with medium heat to get hot.
2. Add 1/4 cup of pancake batter onto the hot skillet and cook until bubbles begin to form on the top. Flip and cook until set. Repeat until your batter is done well. Add your toppings and serve.

Nutrition:
Calories: 231
Protein: 7 g
Carbs: 4.3 g
Fat: 4 g
Sodium: 0mg
Potassium: 265mg

15. Peanut Butter and Banana Breakfast Smoothie

Preparation time: 15 minutes
Cooking time: 0 minutes
Servings: 1

Ingredients:
- 1 cup non-fat milk
- 1 tbsp. peanut butter
- 1 banana
- 1/2 tsp. vanilla

Directions:
1. Set non-fat milk, peanut butter, and banana in a blender. Blend until smooth.

Nutrition:

Calories: 295   Carbs: 4.2 g   Sodium: 100 mg
Protein: 133 g   Fat: 8.4 g   Potassium: 143mg

16. No-Bake Breakfast Granola Bars

Preparation time: 15 minutes   Cooking time: 0 minutes   Servings: 18

Ingredients:
- 2 cup oatmeal, old fashioned
- 1/2 cup raisins
- 1/2 cup brown sugar
- 2 1/2 cup corn rice cereal
- 1/2 cup syrup
- 1/2 cup peanut butter
- 1/2 tsp. vanilla

Directions:
1. In a suitable size mixing bowl, mix using a wooden spoon, rice cereal, oatmeal, and raisins. In a saucepan, merge corn syrup and brown sugar. On a medium-high flame, continuously stir the mixture and bring to a boil.
2. On boiling, take away from heat. In a saucepan, set vanilla and peanut into the sugar mixture. Stir until very smooth.
3. Set peanut butter mixture on the cereal and raisins into the mixing bowl and merge, set a mixture into a 9 x 13 baking tin. Allow to cool properly, and cut into bars (18 pcs).

Nutrition:

Calories: 152   Carbs: 2.6 g   Sodium: 90 mg
Protein: 4 g   Fat: 4.3 g   Potassium: 189mg

17. Mushroom Shallot Frittata

Preparation time: 15 minutes   Cooking time: 25 minutes   Servings: 4

Ingredients:
- 1 tsp. butter
- 4 shallots, chopped
- 1/2 lb. mushrooms, chopped
- 2 tsp. parsley, chopped
- 1 tsp. thyme, dried
- Black pepper
- 3 medium eggs
- 5 large egg whites
- 1 tbsp. milk
- 1/4 cup parmesan cheese, grated

Directions:
1. Heat oven to 350F. In a suitable size oven-proof skillet, warmth butter over medium flame. Attach shallots and sauté for about 5 minutes. Or until golden brown. Set to pot, mushroom, parsley, chopped thyme, and black pepper to flavor.
2. Whisk milk, parmesan, egg whites and eggs into a bowl. Spill the mixture into the skillet, carefully that the mushroom will be covered completely. Transfer the skillet to the oven as soon as the edges begin to set.
3. Bake for 15-20 minutes.

Nutrition:

Calories: 346   Carbs: 48.3 g   Sodium: 18 mg
Protein: 19.1 g   Fat: 12 g   Potassium: 237mg

18. Jack-o-Lantern Pancakes

Preparation time: 15 minutes Cooking time: 5 minutes Servings: 8

Ingredients:
- 1 egg
- 1/2 cup pumpkin, canned
- 1 3/4 cup low-fat milk
- 2 tbsp. vegetable oil
- 2 cup flour
- 2 tbsp. brown sugar
- 1 tbsp. baking powder
- 1 tsp. pumpkin pie spice
- 1/4 tsp. Salt

Directions:
1. In a mixing bowl, merge milk, pumpkin, eggs, and oil. Attach dry ingredients to the egg mixture. Stir gently. Glaze skillet lightly with cooking spray and heat on medium.
2. When the skillet is hot, set batter onto the skillet. When bubbles start bursting, flip pancakes over and cook until golden-brown color.

Nutrition:
Calories: 313   Carbs: 2.8 g   Sodium: 1 mg
Protein: 15 g   Fat: 16 g   Potassium: 120mg

19. Fruit Pizza

Preparation time: 15 minutes Cooking time: 0 minutes Servings: 2

Ingredients:
- 1 English muffin
- 2 tbsp. fat-free cream cheese
- 2 tbsp. strawberries, sliced
- 2 tbsp. blueberries
- 2 tbsp. pineapple, crushed

Directions:
1. Divide English muffin in half and toast halves until slightly browned.
2. Coat both halves with cream cheese. Set fruits atop cream cheese on muffin halves.
3. Serve soon after preparation.

Nutrition:
Calories: 119   Carbs: 2.3 g   Sodium: 28 mg
Protein: 6 g   Fat: 1 g   Potassium: 180mg

20. Flax Banana Yogurt Muffins

Preparation time: 15 minutes Cooking time: 20 minutes Servings: 12

Ingredients:
- 1 cup whole wheat flour
- 1 cup old-fashioned oats, rolled
- 1 tsp. baking soda
- 2 tbsp. flaxseed, ground
- 3 large ripe bananas
- 1/2 cup Greek yogurt
- 1/4 cup applesauce, unsweetened
- 1/4 cup brown sugar
- 2 tsp. vanilla extract

Directions:
1. Set oven at 355F and preheat. Prepare muffin tin, or you can use cooking spray or cupcake liners. Merge dry ingredients in a mixing bowl.
2. In a separate bowl, blend yogurt, banana, sugar, vanilla, and applesauce. Combine both mixtures and mix. Do not over mix. Bake for 20 minutes, or when inserted, toothpick comes out clean.

Nutrition:
Calories: 136   Carbs: 3 g   Sodium: 22 mg
Protein: 4 g   Fat: 2 g   Potassium: 154mg

21. Apple Oats

Preparation time: 5 minutes Cooking time: 5 minutes Servings: 2

Ingredients:
- 1/2 cup oats
- 1 cup water
- 1 apple, chopped
- 1 tsp. olive oil
- 1/2 tsp. vanilla extract

Directions:
1. Spill olive oil in the saucepan and add oats. Cook them for 2 minutes, stir constantly.
2. After this, add water and mix up.
3. Secure the lid and cook oats on low heat for 5 minutes.
4. After this, attach chopped apples and vanilla extract. Stir the meal.

Nutrition:
Calories: 159 Carbs: 2.4 g Sodium: 6 mg
Protein: 3 g Fat: 3.9 g Potassium: 325mg

22. Buckwheat Crepes

Preparation time: 8 minutes Cooking time: 15 minutes Servings: 6

Ingredients:
- 1 cup buckwheat flour
- 1/3 cup whole grain flour
- 1 egg, beaten
- 1 cup skim milk
- 1 tsp. olive oil
- 1/2 tsp. cinnamon, ground

Directions:
1. In the mixing bowl, merge up all ingredients and whisk until you get a smooth batter.
2. Warmth up the non-stick skillet on high heat for 3 minutes.
3. Spill the small amount of batter into the skillet and flatten it in the shape of the crepe.
4. Cook for 1 minute and flip on another side.
5. Redo the same steps with the remaining batter.

Nutrition:
Calories: 122 Carbs: 211 g Sodium: 34 mg
Protein: 5.7 g Fat: 2.2 g Potassium: 393mg

23. Whole Grain Pancakes

Preparation time: 10 minutes Cooking time: 5 minutes Servings: 4

Ingredients:
- 1/2 tsp. baking powder
- 1/4 cup skim milk
- 1 cup whole-grain wheat flour
- 2 tsp. liquid honey
- 1 tsp. olive oil

Directions:
1. Merge up baking powder and flour in the bowl.
2. Add skim milk and olive oil. Whisk the mixture well.
3. Warmth the non-stick skillet and pour the small amount of dough inside in the shape of the pancake. Cook for 2 minutes until the pancake is golden brown.
4. Top the cooked pancakes with liquid honey.

Nutrition:
Calories: 129 Carbs: 5.7 g Sodium: 10 mg
Protein: 4.6 g Fat: 1.7 g Potassium: 189mg

24. Granola Parfait

Preparation time: 10 minutes Cooking time: 0 minutes Servings: 2

Ingredients:
- 1/2 cup low-fat yogurt
- 4 tbsp. granola

Directions:
1. Put 1/2 tbsp. of granola in every glass.
2. Then add 2 tbsp. of low-fat yogurt.
3. Redo the steps till you use all ingredients.
4. Set the parfait in the fridge for up to 2 hours.

Nutrition:
Calories: 79 Carbs: 20.6 g Sodium: 51 mg
Protein: 8 g Fat: 8.1 g Potassium: 134mg

25. Curry Tofu Scramble

Preparation time: 10 minutes Cooking time: 5 minutes Servings: 3

Ingredients:
- 12 oz. tofu, crumbled
- 1 tsp. olive oil
- 1 tsp. curry powder
- 1/4 tsp. chili flakes
- 1/4 cup skim milk

Directions:
1. Heat up olive oil in the skillet.
2. Add crumbled tofu and chili flakes.
3. In the bowl, merge up curry powder and skim milk.
4. Spill the liquid over the crumbled tofu and stir well.
5. Cook the scrambled tofu on medium-high heat.

Nutrition:
Calories: 102 Carbs: 3.3 g Sodium: 25 mg
Protein: 10 g Fat: 6.4 g Potassium: 121mg

26. Easy Veggie Muffins

Preparation time: 10 minutes Cooking time: 40 minutes Servings: 4

Ingredients:
- 3/4 cup cheddar cheese, shredded
- 1 cup biscuit mix
- 1 cup green onion, chopped
- 4 eggs
- 1 cup tomatoes, chopped
- Cooking spray
- 1 cup broccoli, chopped
- 1 tsp. Italian seasoning
- 2 cups non-fat milk
- A pinch black pepper

Directions:
1. Set a muffin tray with cooking spray and divide broccoli, tomatoes, cheese, and onions in each muffin cup.
2. In a bowl, merge green onions with milk, biscuit mix, eggs, pepper, and Italian seasoning, whisk well and pour into the muffin tray as well.
3. Set the muffins in the oven at 375F for 40 minutes, divide them between plates, and serve.

Nutrition:
Calories: 80 Protein: 15 g Sodium: 25 mg
Carbs: 3 g Fat: 5 g Potassium: 156mg

27. Carrot Muffins

Preparation time: 10 minutes Cooking time: 30 minutes Servings: 5
Ingredients:
- 1 and 1/2 cups whole wheat flour
- 1/2 cup stevia
- 1 tsp. baking powder
- 1/2 tsp. cinnamon powder
- 1/2 tsp. baking soda
- 1/4 cup natural apple juice
- 1/4 cup olive oil
- 1 egg
- 1 cup fresh cranberries
- 2 carrots, grated
- 2 tsp. ginger, grated
- 1/4 cup pecans, chopped
- Cooking spray

Directions:
1. Mix the flour with the stevia, baking powder, cinnamon, and baking soda in a large bowl. Attach apple juice, oil, egg, cranberries, carrots, ginger, and pecans and stir well.
2. Oil a muffin tray with cooking spray, divide the muffin mix, put in the oven, and cook at 375F within 30 minutes. Set the muffins between plates and serve for breakfast.

Nutrition:
Calories: 34 Fat: 1 g Sodium: 52 mg
Carbs: 6 g Protein: 0 g Potassium: 120mg

28. Pineapple Oatmeal

Preparation time: 10 minutes Cooking time: 25 minutes Servings: 4
Ingredients:
- 2 cups old-fashioned oats
- 1 cup walnuts, chopped
- 2 cups pineapple, cubed
- 1 tbsp. ginger, grated
- 2 cups non-fat milk
- 2 eggs
- 2 tbsp. stevia
- 2 tsp. vanilla extract

Directions:
1. In a bowl, merge the oats with the pineapple, walnuts, and ginger, stir and divide into 4 ramekins.
2. Mix the milk with the eggs, stevia, and vanilla in a bowl and pour over the oats mix. Bake at 400F within 25 minutes. Serve for breakfast.

Nutrition:
Calories: 200 Fat: 1 g Sodium: 15 mg
Carbs: 4 g Protein: 3 g Potassium: 120mg

29. Spinach Muffins

Preparation time: 10 minutes Cooking time: 30 minutes Servings: 6
Ingredients:
- 6 eggs
- 1/2 cup non-fat milk
- 1 cup low-fat cheese, crumbled
- 4 oz. spinach
- 1/2 cup red pepper, roasted and chopped
- 2 oz. prosciutto, chopped
- Cooking spray

Directions:
1. Mix the eggs with the milk, cheese, spinach, red pepper, and prosciutto in a bowl.
2. Set a muffin tray with cooking spray, divide the muffin mix, introduce in the oven, and bake at 350F within 30 minutes.
3. Divide between plates and serve for breakfast.

Nutrition:
Calories: 112 Fat: 3 g Sodium: 44 mg
Carbs: 1.9 g Protein: 2 g Potassium: 140mg

30. Chia Seeds Breakfast Mix

Preparation time: 8 hours   Cooking time: 0 minutes   Servings: 4
Ingredients:
- 2 cups oats, old-fashioned
- 4 tbsp. chia seeds
- 4 tbsp. coconut sugar
- 3 cups coconut milk
- 1 tsp. lemon zest, grated
- 1 cup blueberries

Directions:
1. In a bowl, merge the oats with chia seeds, sugar, milk, lemon zest, and blueberries, stir, divide into cups and set in the fridge for 8 hours.
2. Serve.

Nutrition:
Calories: 69   Fat: 5 g   Sodium: 0 mg
Carbs: 0 g   Protein: 3 g   Potassium: 145mg

31. Breakfast Fruits Bowls

Preparation time: 10 minutes   Cooking time: 0 minutes   Servings: 2
Ingredients:
- 1 cup mango, chopped
- 1 banana, sliced
- 1 cup pineapple, chopped
- 1 cup almond milk

Directions:
1. Mix the mango with the banana, pineapple, and almond milk in a bowl, stir, divide into smaller bowls, and serve.

Nutrition:
Calories: 10   Fat: 1 g   Sodium: 0mg
Carbs: 0 g   Protein: 0 g   Potassium: 176mg

32. Pumpkin Cookies

Preparation time: 10 minutes   Cooking time: 25 minutes   Servings: 6
Ingredients:
- 2 cups whole wheat flour
- 1 cup oats, old-fashioned
- 1 tsp. baking soda
- 1 tsp. pumpkin pie spice
- 15 oz. pumpkin puree
- 1 cup coconut oil, melted
- 1 cup coconut sugar
- 1 egg
- 1/2 cup pepitas, roasted
- 1/2 cup cherries, dried

Directions:
1. Mix the flour the oats, baking soda, pumpkin spice, pumpkin puree, oil, sugar, egg, pepitas, and cherries in a bowl, stir well, shape medium cookies out of this mix, arrange them all on a baking sheet, then bake within 25 minutes at 350F.
2. Serve the cookies for breakfast.

Nutrition:
Calories: 150   Fat: 8 g   Sodium: 10 mg
Carbs: 24 g   Protein: 1 g   Potassium: 122mg

33. Veggie Scramble

Preparation time: 10 minutes   Cooking time: 2 minutes   Servings: 1
Ingredients:
- 1 egg
- 1 tbsp. water
- 1/4 cup broccoli, chopped
- 1/4 cup mushrooms, chopped

- A pinch black pepper
- 1 tbsp. low-fat mozzarella, shredded
- 1 tbsp. walnuts, chopped
- Cooking spray

Directions:
1. Grease a ramekin with cooking spray, add the egg, water, pepper, mushrooms, and broccoli, and whisk well. Set in the microwave and process for 2 minutes. Attach mozzarella and walnuts on top and serve for breakfast.

Nutrition:
Calories: 128   Fat: 0 g   Sodium: 86 mg
Carbs: 24 g   Protein: 9 g   Potassium: 110mg

34. Mushrooms and Turkey Breakfast

Preparation time: 10 minutes   Cooking time: 1 hour and 5 minutes   Servings: 12

Ingredients:
- 8 oz. whole-wheat bread, cubed
- 12 oz. turkey sausage, chopped
- 2 cups fat-free milk
- 5 oz. low-fat cheddar, shredded
- 3 eggs
- 1/2 cup green onions, chopped
- 1 cup mushrooms, chopped
- 1/2 tsp. sweet paprika
- A pinch black pepper
- 2 tbsp. low-fat parmesan, grated

Directions:
1. Put the bread cubes on a prepared lined baking sheet, bake at 400°F for 8 minutes. Meanwhile, heat a pan over medium-high heat, attach turkey sausage, stir, and brown for 7 minutes.
2. In a bowl, merge the milk with the cheddar, eggs, parmesan, black pepper, and paprika, and whisk well.
3. Attach mushrooms, sausage, bread cubes, and green onions, stir, pour into a baking dish, and bake at 350F within 50 minutes. 5. Slice, divide between plates and serve for breakfast.

Nutrition:
Calories: 88   Fat: 9 g   Sodium: 74 mg
Carbs: 1 g   Protein: 1 g   Potassium: 167mg

35. Mushrooms and Cheese Omelet

Preparation time: 10 minutes   Cooking time: 15 minutes   Servings: 4

Ingredients:
- 2 tbsp. olive oil
- A pinch black pepper
- 3 oz. mushrooms, sliced
- 1 cup baby spinach, chopped
- 3 eggs, whisked
- 2 tbsp. low-fat cheese, grated
- 1 small avocado, peeled, pitted, and cubed
- 1 tbsp. parsley, chopped

Directions:
1. Attach mushrooms, stir, cook them for 5 minutes and transfer to a bowl on a heated pan with the oil over medium-high heat.
2. Warmth up the same pan over medium-high heat, add eggs and black pepper, spread into the pan, cook within 7 minutes, and transfer to a plate.
3. Spill spinach, mushrooms, avocado, and cheese on half of the omelet, wrap up the other half over this mix, set parsley on top, and serve.

Nutrition:
Calories: 136   Fat: 5 g   Sodium: 82 mg
Carbs: 5 g   Protein: 16 g   Potassium: 129mg

Chapter 4. Lunch

36. Gnocchi with Tomato Basil Sauce

Preparation time: 15 minutes   Cooking time: 25 minutes   Servings: 6

Ingredients:
- 2 tbsp. olive oil
- 1/2 yellow onion, peeled and diced
- 3 cloves garlic, peeled and minced
- 1 (32-oz.) can no-salt-added San Marzano tomatoes, crushed
- 1/4 cup fresh basil leaves
- 2 tsp. Italian seasoning
- 1/4 tsp. Kosher or sea salt
- 1 tsp. sugar, granulated
- 1/2 tsp. black pepper, ground
- 1/8 tsp. red pepper flakes, crushed
- 1 tbsp. heavy cream (optional)
- 12 oz. gnocchi
- 1/4 cup Parmesan cheese, freshly grated

Directions:
1. Warmth up the olive oil in stockpot over medium heat. Add the onion and sauté for 5 to 6 minutes, until soft. Stir in the garlic and stir until fragrant, 30 to 60 seconds. Then stir in the tomatoes, basil, Italian seasoning, salt, sugar, black pepper, and crushed red pepper flakes.
2. Bring to a simmer for 15 minutes. Stir in the heavy cream, if desired. For a smooth, puréed sauce, use an immersion blender or transfer sauce to a blender and purée until smooth. Taste and adjust the seasoning, if necessary.
3. While the sauce simmers, cook the gnocchi according to the package instructions, remove with a slotted spoon, and transfer to 6 bowls. Pour the sauce over the gnocchi and top with the Parmesan cheese.

Nutrition:
Calories: 287   Fat: 7 g   Protein: 10 g
Carbs: 4.1 g   Sodium: 27 mg   Potassium: 140mg

37. Creamy Pumpkin Pasta

Preparation time: 15 minutes   Cooking time: 30 minutes   Servings: 6

Ingredients:
- 1-lb. whole-grain linguine
- 1 tbsp. olive oil
- 3 garlic cloves, peeled and minced
- 2 tbsp. fresh sage, chopped
- 1 1/2 cups pumpkin purée
- 1 cup vegetable stock, unsalted
- 1/2 cup low-fat evaporated milk
- 1/4 tsp. Kosher or sea salt
- 1/2 tsp. black pepper, ground
- 1/2 tsp. nutmeg, ground
- 1/4 tsp. cayenne pepper, ground
- 1/2 cup Parmesan cheese, divided and freshly grated

Directions:
1. Cook the whole-grain linguine in a large pot of boiled water. Reserve 1/2 cup of pasta water and drain the rest. Set the pasta aside.
2. Warm-up the olive oil over medium heat in a large skillet. Add the garlic and sage and sauté for 1 to 2 minutes, until soft and fragrant. Whisk in the pumpkin purée, stock, milk, and reserved pasta water and simmer for 4 to 5 minutes, until thickened.
3. Whisk in the salt, black pepper, nutmeg, and cayenne pepper, and half of the Parmesan cheese. Stir in the cooked whole-grain linguine. Evenly divide the pasta among 6 bowls and top with the remaining Parmesan cheese.

Nutrition:
Calories: 381   Fat: 8 g   Protein: 15 g
Carbs: 6.3 g   Sodium: 75 mg   Potassium: 130mg

38. Mexican-Style Potato Casserole

Preparation time: 15 minutes Cooking time: 60 minutes Servings: 8

Ingredients:
- Cooking spray
- 2 tbsp. canola oil
- 1/2 yellow onion, peeled and diced
- 4 garlic cloves, peeled and minced
- 2 tbsp. all-purpose flour
- 1 1/4 cups milk
- 1 tbsp. chili powder
- 1/2 tbsp. cumin, ground
- 1/4 tsp. Kosher salt or sea salt
- 1/2 tsp. black pepper, ground
- 1/4 tsp. cayenne pepper, ground
- 1 1/2 cups Mexican-style cheese, shredded and divided
- 1 (4-oz.) can green chilies, drained
- 1 1/2 lb. baby Yukon Gold or red potatoes, thinly sliced
- 1 red bell pepper, thinly sliced

Directions:
1. Preheat the oven to 400F. Oil a 9-x-13-inch baking dish. In a large saucepan, warm canola oil on medium heat. Attach the onion and sauté for 4 to 5 minutes, until soft. Mix in the garlic, then cook until fragrant, 30 to 60 seconds.
2. Mix in the flour, then put in the milk while whisking. Slow simmer for about 5 minutes, until thickened. Whisk in the chili powder, cumin, salt, black pepper, and cayenne pepper.
3. Remove from the heat and whisk in half of the shredded cheese and the green chilies. Taste and adjust the seasoning, if necessary. Line up one-third of the sliced potatoes and sliced bell pepper in the baking dish and top with a quarter of the remaining shredded cheese.
4. Repeat with 2 more layers. Pour the cheese sauce over the top and sprinkle with the remaining shredded cheese. Cover it with aluminum foil and bake within 45 to 50 minutes, until the potatoes are tender.
5. Remove the foil and bake again within 5 to 10 minutes, until the topping is slightly browned. Let cool within 20 minutes before slicing into 8 pieces. Serve.

Nutrition:
Calories: 195 Fat: 10 g Protein: 8 g
Carbs: 1.9 g Sodium: 47 mg Potassium: 160mg

39. Black Bean Stew with Cornbread

Preparation time: 15 minutes Cooking time: 55 minutes Servings: 6

Ingredients:
For the black bean stew:
- 2 tbsp. canola oil
- 1 yellow onion, peeled and diced
- 4 garlic cloves, peeled and minced
- 1 tbsp. chili powder
- 1 tbsp. cumin, ground
- 1/4 tsp. Kosher or sea salt
- 1/2 tsp. black pepper, ground
- 2 cans no-salt-added black beans, drained
- 1 (10-oz.) can tomatoes, fire-roasted, diced
- 1/2 cup fresh cilantro leaves, chopped

For the cornbread topping:
- 1 1/4 cups cornmeal
- 1/2 cup all-purpose flour
- 1/2 tsp. baking powder
- 1/4 tsp. baking soda
- 1/8 tsp. Kosher or sea salt
- 1 cup low-fat buttermilk
- 2 tbsp. honey
- 1 large egg

Directions:
1. Warm-up the canola oil over medium heat in a large Dutch oven or stockpot. Add the onion and sauté for 4 to 6 minutes, until the onion is soft. Stir in the garlic, chili powder, cumin, salt, and black pepper.
2. Cook within 1 to 2 minutes, until fragrant. Add the black beans and diced tomatoes. Bring to a simmer and cook for 15 minutes. Remove, then stir in the fresh cilantro. Taste and adjust the seasoning, if necessary.
3. Preheat the oven to 375°F. While the stew simmers, prepare the cornbread topping. Mix the cornmeal, baking soda, flour, baking powder, plus salt in a bowl. In a measuring cup, whisk the buttermilk, honey, and egg until combined. Put the batter into the dry fixing until just combined.
4. In oven-safe bowls or dishes, spoon out the black bean soup. Distribute dollops of the cornbread batter on top and then spread it out evenly with a spatula. Bake within 30 minutes, until the cornbread is just set.

Nutrition:
Calories: 359
Carbs: 6.1 g
Fat: 7 g
Sodium: 19 mg
Protein: 14 g
Potassium: 132mg

40. Mushroom Florentine

Preparation time: 15 minutes   Cooking time: 20 minutes   Servings: 4

Ingredients:
- 5 oz. whole-grain pasta
- 1/4 cup low-sodium vegetable broth
- 1 cup mushrooms, sliced
- 1/4 cup soy milk
- 1 tsp. olive oil
- 1/2 tsp. Italian seasonings

Directions:
1. Process the pasta according to the direction of the manufacturer. Then pour olive oil into the saucepan and heat it. Attach mushrooms and Italian seasonings. Set the mushrooms well and cook for 10 minutes.
2. Then add soy milk and vegetable broth. Set cooked pasta and mix up the mixture well. Process it for 5 minutes on low heat.

Nutrition:
Calories: 287
Carbs: 5.4 g
Protein: 12.4 g
Fat: 4.2 g
Sodium: 26 mg
Potassium: 146mg

41. Hassel back Eggplant

Preparation time: 15 minutes   Cooking time: 25 minutes   Servings: 2

Ingredients:
- 2 eggplants, trimmed
- 2 tomatoes, sliced
- 1 tbsp. low-fat yogurt
- 1 tsp. curry powder
- 1 tsp. olive oil

Directions:
1. Set the cuts in the eggplants in the shape of the Hassel back. Then set the vegetables with curry powder and fill with sliced tomatoes.
2. Spill the eggplants with olive oil and yogurt and wrap in the foil (each Hassel back eggplant wrap separately).
3. Process the vegetables at 375F for 25 minutes.

Nutrition:
Calories: 188
Protein: 7 g
Carbs: 3.1 g
Fat: 3 g
Sodium: 23 mg
Potassium: 137mg

42. Vegetarian Kebabs

Preparation time: 15 minutes Cooking time: 6 minutes Servings: 4

Ingredients:
- 2 tbsp. balsamic vinegar
- 1 tbsp. olive oil
- 1 tsp. parsley, dried
- 2 tbsp. water
- 2 sweet peppers
- 2 red onions, peeled
- 2 zucchinis, trimmed

Directions:
1. Divide the sweet peppers and onions into medium size squares. Then slice the zucchini. String all vegetables into the skewers. After this, in the shallow bowl, merge up olive oil, dried parsley, water, and balsamic vinegar.
2. Spill the vegetable skewers with olive oil mixture and transfer in the preheated to 390F grill. Cook the kebabs within 3 minutes per side or until the vegetables are light brown.

Nutrition:
Calories: 88 Protein: 2.4 g Sodium: 14 mg
Carbs: 13 g Fat: 3.9 g Potassium: 122mg

43. White Beans Stew

Preparation time: 15 minutes Cooking time: 55 minutes Servings: 4

Ingredients:
- 1 cup white beans, soaked
- 1 cup low-sodium vegetable broth
- 1 cup zucchini, chopped
- 1 tsp. tomato paste
- 1 tbsp. avocado oil
- 4 cups water
- 1/2 tsp. peppercorns
- 1/2 tsp. black pepper, ground
- 1/4 tsp. nutmeg, ground

Directions:
1. Heat avocado oil in the saucepan, add zucchinis, and roast them for 5 minutes. After this, add white beans, vegetable broth, tomato paste, water, peppercorns, ground black pepper, and ground nutmeg.
2. Simmer the stew within 50 minutes on low heat.

Nutrition:
Calories: 184 Carbs: 3.6 g Sodium: 5 mg
Protein: 12.3 g Fat: 1 g Potassium: 142mg

44. Vegetarian Lasagna

Preparation time: 15 minutes Cooking time: 30 minutes Servings: 6

Ingredients:
- 1 cup carrot, diced
- 1/2 cup bell pepper, diced
- 1 cup spinach, chopped
- 1 tbsp. olive oil
- 1 tsp. chili powder
- 1 cup tomatoes, chopped
- 4 oz. low-fat cottage cheese
- 1 eggplant, sliced
- 1 cup low-sodium vegetable broth

Directions:
1. Put carrot, bell pepper, and spinach in the saucepan. Add olive oil and chili powder and stir the vegetables well. Cook them for 5 minutes.
2. Make the sliced eggplant layer in the casserole mold and top it with a vegetable mixture. Add tomatoes, vegetable stock, and cottage cheese. Bake the lasagna for 30 minutes at 375F.

Nutrition:
Calories: 77 Carbs: 9.7 g Sodium: 24 mg
Protein: 4.1 g Fat: 3 g Potassium: 187mg

45. Pan-Fried Salmon with Salad

Preparation time: 15 minutes Cooking time: 20 minutes Servings: 4

Ingredients:
- Pinch salt and pepper
- 1 tbsp. extra-virgin olive oil
- 2 tbsp. butter, unsalted
- 1/2 tsp. fresh dill
- 1 tbsp. fresh lemon juice
- 100g salad leaves, or bag of mixed leaves

Salad Dressing:
- 3 tbsp. olive oil
- 2 tbsp. balsamic vinaigrette
- 1/2 tsp. maple syrup (honey)

Directions:
1. Pat-dry the salmon fillets with a paper towel and season with a pinch of salt and pepper. In a skillet, warm-up oil over medium-high heat and add fillets. Cook each side within 5 to 7 minutes until golden brown.
2. Dissolve butter, dill, and lemon juice in a small saucepan. Put the butter mixture onto the cooked salmon. Lastly, combine all the salad dressing ingredients and drizzle to mixed salad leaves in a large bowl. Toss to coat. Serve with fresh salads on the side. Enjoy!

Nutrition:
Calories: 307 Fat: 22 g Sodium: 80 mg
Carbs: 1.7 g Protein: 34.6 g Potassium: 192mg

46. Veggie Variety

Preparation time: 15 minutes Cooking time: 15 minutes Servings: 2

Ingredients:
- 1/2 onion, diced
- 1 tsp. vegetable oil (corn or sunflower oil)
- 200 g Tofu/bean curd
- 4 cherry tomatoes, halved
- 30ml vegetable milk (soy or oat milk)
- 1/2 tsp. curry powder
- 0.25 tsp. paprika
- Pinch Salt and Pepper
- 2 slices Vegan protein bread/ Whole grain bread
- Chives, for garnish

Directions:
1. Dice the onion and fry in a frying pan with the oil. Break the tofu by hand into small pieces and put them in the pan. Sauté 7-8 min.
2. Season with curry, paprika, salt, and pepper. The cherry tomatoes and milk and cook it all over roast a few minutes.
3. Serve with bread as desired and sprinkle with chopped chives.

Nutrition:
Calories: 216 Fat: 8.4 g Sodium: 40 mg
Carbs: 24.8 g Protein: 14.1 g Potassium: 189mg

47. Vegetable Pasta

Preparation time: 15 minutes Cooking time: 15 minutes Servings: 4

Ingredients:
- 1 kg thin zucchini
- 20 g fresh ginger
- 350g tofu, smoked
- 1 lime
- 2 cloves garlic
- 2 tbsp. sunflower oil
- 2 tbsp. sesame seeds
- Pinch salt and pepper
- 4 tbsp. onions, fried

Directions:
1. Wash and clean the zucchini and, using a julienne cutter, cut the pulp around the kernel into long thin strips (noodles). Ginger peel and finely chop. Crumble tofu. Halve lime, squeeze juice. Peel and chop garlic.
2. Warm-up 1 tbsp. of oil in a pan and process the tofu for about 5 minutes. After about 3 minutes, add ginger, garlic, and sesame. Season with soy sauce. Remove from the pan and keep warm.
3. Wipe out the pan, then warm 2 tbsp. of oil in it. Stir fry zucchini strips for about 4 minutes while turning. Season with salt, pepper, and lime juice. Arrange pasta and tofu. Sprinkle with fried onions.

Nutrition:
Calories: 262 Fat: 17.7 g Sodium: 62 mg
Carbs: 7.1 g Protein: 15.4 g Potassium: 134mg

48. Vegetable Noodles with Bolognese

Preparation time: 15 minutes Cooking time: 15 minutes Servings: 4
Ingredients:
- 1 kg small zucchini (e.g., green and yellow)
- 600 g carrots
- 1 onion
- 1 tbsp. olive oil
- 250 g beef steak
- Pinch Salt and pepper
- 2 tbsp. tomato paste
- 1 tbsp. flour
- 1 tsp. vegetable broth (instant)
- 40 g pecorino or parmesan cheese
- 1 small potty of basil

Directions:
1. Clean and peel zucchini and carrots and wash. Using a sharp, long knife, cut first into thin slices, then into long, fine strips. Clean or peel the soup greens, wash and cut into tiny cubes. Peel the onion and chop finely. Heat the Bolognese oil in a large pan. Fry hack in it crumbly. Season with salt and pepper.
2. Briefly sauté the prepared vegetable and onion cubes. Stir in tomato paste. Dust the flour, sweat briefly. Spill in 400 ml of water and stir in the vegetable stock. Boil everything, simmer for 7-8 minutes.
3. Meanwhile, cook the vegetable strips in plenty of salted water for 3-5 minutes. Drain, collecting some cooking water. Add the vegetable strips to the pan and mix well. If the sauce is not liquid enough, stir in some vegetable cooking water and season everything again.
4. Slicing cheese into fine shavings. Wash the basil, shake dry, peel off the leaves, and cut roughly. Arrange vegetable noodles, sprinkle with parmesan and basil

Nutrition:
Calories: 269 Fat: 9.7 g Sodium: 53 mg
Carbs: 1.7 g Protein: 25.6 g Potassium: 172mg

49. Black Bean Burgers with Lettuce "Buns"

Preparation time: 20 minutes Cooking time: 10 minutes Servings: 4
Ingredients:
- 1/2 cup uncooked brown rice
- 3 cups canned low-sodium black beans, drained and rinsed
- 1/4 cup brown rice flour
- 1/2 large red onion, chopped
- 1 large red bell pepper, diced
- 1/2 cup chopped fresh cilantro
- 1 teaspoon chili powder
- 1 teaspoon freshly ground black pepper
- 1/4 teaspoon sea salt
- 1 medium Hass avocado, sliced
- 1 tomato, sliced
- 1 head Boston lettuce

Directions:
1. Preheat the air fryer to 350F. Process the brown rice according to the package directions.
2. Mash the black beans in a large bowl until they are broken up, leaving some whole beans visible.
3. Stir in the brown rice, rice flour, onion, bell pepper, cilantro, chili powder, black pepper, and salt until evenly combined. Transfer to the refrigerator for 5 minutes to chill so that it is easier to form into patties.
4. Set the bean mixture into 4 patties, about 5 inches in diameter.
5. Working in batches if necessary, place the burgers in a single layer in the air fryer basket and cook for 8 minutes. Toss them over and cook until golden brown.
6. To assemble, top each black bean patty with one-quarter of the avocado and tomato slices. Using 2 or 3 lettuce leaves per patty, wrap the leaves around the patty as tightly as you can.

Nutrition:
Calories: 452
Carbs: 27.6 g
Fat: 22.3 g
Protein: 37.1 g
Sodium: 39 mg
Potassium: 175mg

50. Curry Vegetable Noodles with Chicken

Preparation time: 15 minutes Cooking time: 15 minutes Servings: 2
Ingredients:
- 600g zucchini
- 500g chicken fillet
- Pinch salt and pepper
- 2 tbsp. oil
- 150 g red and yellow cherry tomatoes
- 1 tsp. curry powder
- 150g Fat-free cheese
- 200 ml vegetable broth
- 4 stalks fresh basil

Directions:
1. Wash the zucchini, clean, and cut into long thin strips with a spiral cutter. Wash meat, pat dry, and season with salt. Heat 1 tbsp. oil in a pan. Roast chicken in it for about 10 minutes until golden brown.
2. Wash cherry tomatoes and cut in half. Approximately 3 minutes before the end of the cooking time to the chicken in the pan. Heat 1 tbsp. oil in another pan. Sweat curry powder into it then stirs in cream cheese and broth. Flavor the sauce with salt plus pepper and simmer for about 4 minutes.
3. Wash the basil, shake it dry and pluck the leaves from the stems. Cut small leaves of 3 stems. Remove meat from the pan and cut it into strips. Add tomatoes, basil, and zucchini to the sauce and heat for 2-3 minutes. Serve vegetable noodles and meat on plates and garnish with basil.

Nutrition:
Calories: 376
Carbs: 9.5 g
Fat: 17.2 g
Protein: 44.9 g
Sodium: 29 mg
Potassium: 152mg

51. Tempeh Veggie Tacos

Preparation time: 10 minutes Cooking time: 10 minutes Servings: 4
Ingredients:
- 12 ounces tempeh, cut into cubes
- 1 tablespoon chili powder
- 1/2 teaspoon paprika
- 1/2 teaspoon ground cumin
- 1/4 teaspoon sea salt
- 1 tablespoon freshly squeezed lime juice
- Extra-virgin olive oil cooking spray bottle
- 1 cup chopped romaine lettuce
- 8 (6-inch) corn tortillas
- 1 bell pepper, chopped
- 1/2 cup chopped fresh cilantro
- 1 medium Hass avocado
- 1 jalapeño, sliced (optional)

Directions:
1. Preheat the air fryer to 325F.
2. In a medium bowl, stir together the tempeh, chili powder, paprika, cumin, salt, and lime juice.
3. Working in batches if necessary, arrange the tempeh wedges in a single layer in the air fryer basket, ensuring not to crowd them. Mist with the olive oil and cook for 10 minutes, or until the tempeh is browned and slightly crispy on the outside.
4. To assemble the tacos, layer the lettuce on the bottom of each tortilla. Top with the tempeh, bell pepper, cilantro, avocado, and jalapeño slices (if using).

Nutrition:
Calories: 262
Fat: 17.7g
Carbs: 7.1g
Protein: 15.4g
Sodium: 62mg
Potassium: 137mg

52. Chickpea Frittata with Tomatoes and Watercress

Preparation time: 5 minutes   Cooking time: 10 minutes   Servings: 4

Ingredients:
- 2 cups chickpea flour
- 3 tablespoons nutritional yeast
- 1/2 teaspoon baking powder
- 2 cups filtered water
- 1/4 teaspoon sea salt
- 1 large bell pepper, chopped
- 12 ounces cherry tomatoes, chopped
- 2 cups chopped baby kale
- Extra-virgin olive oil cooking spray
- 1 cup watercress or pea shoots

Directions:
1. In a large bowl, set together the chickpea flour, nutritional yeast, baking powder, and water until smooth. Stir in the salt, bell pepper, tomatoes, and kale.
2. Working in batches if necessary, mist an air fryer baking pan with the olive oil, add the chickpea mixture, and smooth to an even layer. Place the pan in the air fryer basket and set the temperature to 375°F. Cook for 10 minutes, or until a toothpick inserted in the center comes out clean.
3. Top with the watercress and serve immediately.

Nutrition:
Calories: 269
Fat: 9.7g
Carbs: 21.7g
Protein: 25.6g
Sodium: 53mg
Potassium: 182mg

53. Harissa Bolognese with Vegetable Noodles

Preparation time: 15 minutes   Cooking time: 30 minutes   Servings: 4

Ingredients:
- 2 onions
- 1 clove of garlic
- 3-4 tbsp. oil
- 400g ground beef
- Pinch salt, pepper, cinnamon
- 1 tsp. Harissa (Arabic seasoning paste, tube)
- 1 tablespoon tomato paste
- 2 sweet potatoes
- 2 medium zucchini
- 3 stems/basil
- 100g of feta

Directions:
1. Peel onions and garlic, finely dice. Warm-up 1 tbsp of oil in a wide saucepan. Fry hack in it crumbly. Fry onions and garlic for a short time. Season with salt, pepper, and 1/2 teaspoon cinnamon. Stir in harissa and tomato paste.
2. Add tomatoes and 200ml of water, bring to the boil and simmer for about 15 minutes with occasional stirring. Peel sweet potatoes and zucchini or clean and wash. Cut vegetables into spaghetti with a spiral cutter.
3. Warm-up 2-3 tablespoons of oil in a large pan. Braise sweet potato spaghetti in it for about 3 minutes. Add the zucchini spaghetti and continue to simmer for 3-4 minutes while turning.

4. Season with salt and pepper. Wash the basil, shake dry and peel off the leaves. Garnish vegetable spaghetti and Bolognese on plates. Feta crumbles over. Sprinkle with basil.

Nutrition:
Calories: 452 Carbs: 27.6g Sodium: 13mg
Fat: 22.3g Protein: 37.1g Potassium: 191mg

54. Roasted Apple–Butternut Squash Soup

Preparation time: 20 minutes Cooking time: 35 minutes Servings: 4

Ingredients:
- 2 cups peeled and cubed butternut squash
- 2 cups peeled and cubed sweet potato
- 1 cup peeled and chopped carrots
- 2 shallots, peeled and sliced
- 1 medium apple, cored and slice into 1-inch cubes
- 1 teaspoon ground cinnamon
- Avocado oil cooking spray
- 3 1/2 cups low-sodium vegetable broth

Directions:
1. Preheat the air fryer to 400F.
2. Working in batches if necessary, arrange the butternut squash, sweet potato, carrots, shallots, and apple in a single layer in the basket, being careful not to crowd them. Sprinkle with the cinnamon and mist with the avocado oil.
3. Cook the vegetables for 25 minutes, or until golden brown, shaking or stirring halfway through.
4. Carefully transfer the roasted vegetables to a 4-quart soup pot over medium heat. Add the broth and simmer for about 10 minutes.
5. Remove the soup from the heat and allow to cool slightly, then use an immersion blender or food processor to blend the vegetables until smooth.

Nutrition:
Calories: 376 Carbs: 9.5 Sodium: 32mg
Fat: 17.2g Protein: 44.9g Potassium: 119mg

55. Sweet and Sour Vegetable Noodles

Preparation time: 15 minutes Cooking time: 30 minutes Servings: 4

Ingredients:
- 4 chicken fillets (75 g each)
- 300g of whole wheat spaghetti
- 750g carrots
- 1/2 liter clear chicken broth (instant)
- 1 tablespoon sugar
- 1 tbsp. of green peppercorns
- 2-3 tbsp. balsamic vinegar
- Capuchin flowers
- Pinch of salt

Directions:
1. Cook spaghetti in boiling water for about 8 minutes. Then drain. In the meantime, peel and wash carrots. Cut into long strips (best with a special grater). Set for 2 minutes in boiling salted water, drain. Wash chicken fillets. Add to the boiling chicken soup and cook for about 15 minutes.
2. Melt the sugar until golden brown. Measure 1/4 liter of chicken stock and deglaze the sugar with it. Add peppercorns, cook for 2 minutes. Season with salt and vinegar. Add the fillets, then cut into thin slices. Then turn the pasta and carrots in the sauce and serve garnished with capuchin blossoms. Serve and enjoy.

Nutrition:
Calories: 374 Carbs: 23.1g Sodium: 95 mg
Fat: 21g Protein: 44g Potassium: 133mg

56. Tuna Sandwich

Preparation time: 15 minutes Cooking time: 0 minutes Servings: 1

Ingredients:
- 2 slices whole grain bread
- 1 6-oz. can low sodium tuna in water, in its juice
- 2 tsp. yogurt (1.5% fat) or low-fat mayonnaise
- 1 medium tomato, diced
- 1/2 small sweet onion, finely diced
- Lettuce leaves

Directions:
1. Toast whole grain bread slices. Mix tuna, yogurt, or mayonnaise, diced tomato, and onion. Cover the toasted bread with lettuce leaves and spread the tuna mixture on the sandwich. Spread tuna mixed on toasted bread with lettuce leaves.
2. Place another disc as a cover on top.
3. Enjoy the sandwich.

Nutrition:
Calories: 235 Carbs: 25.9g Sodium: 50mg
Fat: 3g Protein: 27.8g Potassium: 113mg

57. Sweet Potatoes and Zucchini Soup

Preparation time: 10 minutes Cooking time: 20 minutes Servings: 8

Ingredients:
- 4 cups vegetable stock
- 2 tablespoons olive oil
- 2 sweet potatoes, peeled and cubed
- 8 zucchinis, chopped
- 2 yellow onions, chopped
- 1 cup of coconut milk
- A pinch of black pepper
- 1 tablespoon coconut aminos
- 4 tablespoons dill, chopped
- 1/2 teaspoon basil, chopped

Directions:
1. Heat up a pot with the oil over medium heat, add onion, stir and cook for 5 minutes. Add zucchinis, stock, basil, potato, and pepper, stir and cook for 15 minutes more. Add milk, coconut aminos, and dill, pulse using an immersion blender, ladle into bowls and serve for lunch.

Nutrition:
Calories: 270 Fat: 4g Sodium: 16 mg
Carbs: 5g Protein: 11g Potassium: 111mg

58. Lemongrass and Chicken Soup

Preparation time: 10 minutes Cooking time: 25 minutes Servings: 4

Ingredients:
- 4 lime leaves, torn
- 4 cups vegetable stock, low-sodium
- 1 lemongrass stalk, chopped
- 1 tablespoon ginger, grated
- 1 pound chicken breast, skinless, boneless, and cubed
- 8 ounces mushrooms, chopped
- 4 Thai chilies, chopped
- 13 ounces of coconut milk
- 1/4 cup lime juice
- 1/4 cup cilantro, chopped
- A pinch of black pepper

Directions:
1. Put the stock into a pot, bring to a simmer over medium heat, add lemongrass, ginger, and lime leaves, stir, cook for 10 minutes, strain into another pot, and heat up over medium heat again.
2. Add chicken, mushrooms, milk, cilantro, black pepper, chilies, and lime juice, stir, simmer for 15 minutes, ladle into bowls and serve.

Nutrition:

Calories: 105   Fat: 2g   Sodium: 100mg
Carbs: 1g   Protein: 15g   Potassium: 115mg

59. Easy Lunch Salmon Steaks

Preparation time: 10 minutes   Cooking time: 20 minutes   Servings: 4

Ingredients:
- 1 large salmon fillet, cut into 4 steaks
- 3 garlic cloves, minced
- 1 yellow onion, chopped
- Black pepper to taste
- 2 tablespoons olive oil
- 1/4 cup parsley, chopped
- Juice of 1 lemon
- 1 tablespoon thyme, chopped
- 4 cups of water

Directions:
1. Heat a pan with the oil on medium-high heat, cook onion and garlic for 3 minutes.
2. Add black pepper, parsley, thyme, water, and lemon juice, stir, bring to a gentle boil, add salmon steaks, cook them for 15 minutes, drain, divide between plates and serve with a side salad for lunch.

Nutrition:

Calories: 110   Fat: 4g   Sodium: 130 mg
Carbs: 3g   Protein: 15g   Potassium: 110mg

60. Light Balsamic Salad

Preparation time: 10 minutes   Cooking time: 0 minutes   Servings: 3

Ingredients:
- 1 orange, cut into segments
- 2 green onions, chopped
- 1 Romaine lettuce head, torn
- 1 avocado, pitted, peeled, and cubed
- 1/4 cup almonds, sliced

For the salad dressing:
- 1 teaspoon mustard
- 1/4 cup olive oil
- 2 tablespoons balsamic vinegar
- Juice of 1/2 orange
- Salt and black pepper

Directions:
1. In a salad bowl, mix oranges with avocado, lettuce, almonds, and green onions.
2. In another bowl, mix olive oil with vinegar, mustard, orange juice, salt, and pepper, whisk well, add this to your salad, toss and serve.

Nutrition:

Calories: 35   Fat: 2g   Sodium: 70 mg
Carbs: 5g   Protein: 0g   Potassium: 128mg

61. Purple Potato Soup

Preparation time: 10 minutes   Cooking time: 1 hour and 15 minutes   Servings: 6

Ingredients:
- 6 purple potatoes, chopped
- 1 cauliflower head, florets separated
- Black pepper to taste
- 4 garlic cloves, minced
- 1 yellow onion, chopped
- 3 tablespoons olive oil
- 1 tablespoon thyme, chopped
- 1 leek, chopped
- 2 shallots, chopped
- 4 cups chicken stock, low-sodium

Directions:
1. In a baking dish, mix potatoes with onion, cauliflower, garlic, pepper, thyme, and half of the oil, toss to coat, introduce in the oven and bake for 45 minutes at 400F.
2. Heat a pot with the rest of the oil over medium-high heat, add leeks and shallots, stir and cook for 10 minutes.
3. Add roasted veggies and stock, stir, bring to a boil, cook for 20 minutes, transfer soup to your food processor, blend well, divide into bowls, and serve.

Nutrition:
Calories: 70 Fat: 0g Sodium: 6 mg
Carbs: 1/5g Protein: 2g Potassium: 192mg

62. Leeks Soup

Preparation time: 10 minutes Cooking time: 1 hour and 15 minutes Servings: 6

Ingredients:
- 2 gold potatoes, chopped
- 1 cup cauliflower florets
- Black pepper to taste
- 5 leeks, chopped
- 4 garlic cloves, minced
- 1 yellow onion, chopped
- 3 tablespoons olive oil
- Handful parsley, chopped
- 4 cups low-sodium chicken stock

Directions:
1. Heat up a pot with the oil over medium-high heat, add onion and garlic, stir and cook for 5 minutes.
2. Add potatoes, cauliflower, black pepper, leeks, and stock, stir, bring to a simmer, cook over medium heat for 30 minutes, blend using an immersion blender, add parsley, stir, ladle into bowls and serve.

Nutrition:
Calories: 125 Fat: 1g Sodium: 52 mg
Carbs: 2.9g Protein: 4g Potassium: 132mg

63. Cauliflower Lunch Salad

Preparation time: 2 hours Cooking time: 10 minutes Servings: 4

Ingredients:
- 1/3 cup low-sodium vegetable stock
- 2 tablespoons olive oil
- 6 cups cauliflower florets, grated
- Black pepper to taste
- 1/4 cup red onion, chopped
- 1 red bell pepper, chopped
- Juice of 1/2 lemon
- 1/2 cup kalamata olives halved
- 1 teaspoon mint, chopped
- 1 tablespoon cilantro, chopped

Directions:
1. Warmth up a pan with the oil over medium-high heat, add cauliflower, pepper and stock, stir, cook for 10 minutes, place to a bowl, and keep in the fridge for 2 hours.
2. Mix cauliflower with olives, onion, bell pepper, black pepper, mint, cilantro, and lemon juice, toss to coat, and serve.

Nutrition:
Calories: 102 Fat: 10g Sodium: 97 mg
Carbs: 3g Protein: 0g Potassium: 152mg

64. Tofu and Green Bean Stir Fry

Preparation time: 15 minutes Cooking time: 20 minutes Servings: 4

Ingredients:
- 1 14-ounce package extra-firm tofu
- 2 tablespoons canola oil

- 1 pound green beans, chopped
- 2 carrots, peeled and thinly sliced
- 1/2 cup stir fry sauce or store-bought lower-sodium stir fry sauce
- 2 cups fluffy brown rice
- 2 scallions, thinly sliced
- 2 tablespoons sesame seeds

Directions:
1. Put the tofu on your plate lined with a kitchen towel, put a separate kitchen towel over the tofu, and place a heavy pot on top, changing towels every time they become soaked. Set aside for 15 minutes to remove the moisture. Cut the tofu into 1-inch cubes.
2. Heat the canola oil in a large wok or skillet to medium-high heat. Add the tofu cubes and cook, flipping every 1 to 2 minutes, so all sides become browned. Remove from the skillet and place the green beans and carrots in the hot oil. Stir-fry for 4 to 5 minutes, occasionally tossing, until crisp and slightly tender.
3. While the vegetables are cooking, prepare the Stir fry sauce (if using homemade). Place the tofu back in the skillet. Put the sauce over the tofu and vegetables and let simmer for 2 to 3 minutes. Serve over rice, then top with scallions and sesame seeds.

Nutrition:
Calories: 380
Fat: 15g
Sodium: 440mg
Potassium: 454mg
Carbohydrate: 45g
Protein: 16g
Potassium: 182mg

65. Spicy Tofu Burrito Bowls with Cilantro Avocado Sauce

Preparation time: 15 minutes   Cooking time: 15 minutes   Servings: 4

Ingredients:
For the sauce:
- 1/4 cup plain non-fat Greek yogurt
- 1/2 cup fresh cilantro leaves
- 1/2 ripe avocado, peeled
- Zest and juice of 1 lime
- 2 garlic cloves, peeled
- 1/4 teaspoon kosher or sea salt
- 2 tablespoons water

For the burrito bowls:
- 1 14-ounce package extra-firm tofu
- 1 tablespoon canola oil
- 1 yellow or orange bell pepper, diced
- 2 tablespoons taco seasoning
- 1/4 teaspoon kosher or sea salt
- 2 cups fluffy brown rice
- 1 15-ounce can black beans, drained

Directions:
1. Set all the sauce ingredients in the bowl of a food processor or blender and purée until smooth. Taste and adjust the seasoning, if necessary. Refrigerate until ready for use.
2. Put the tofu on your plate lined with a kitchen towel. Put another kitchen towel over the tofu and place a heavy pot on top, changing towels if they become soaked. Let it stand for 15 minutes to remove the moisture. Cut the tofu into 1-inch cubes.
3. Warm-up canola oil in a large skillet over medium heat. Add the tofu and bell pepper and sauté, breaking up the tofu into smaller pieces for 4 to 5 minutes. Stir in the taco seasoning, salt, and 1/4 cup of water. Evenly divide the rice and black beans among 4 bowls. Top with the tofu/bell pepper mixture and top with the cilantro avocado sauce.

Nutrition:
Calories: 383
Fat: 13g
Carbs: 4.8g
Sodium: 138 mg
Protein: 21g
Potassium: 122.6mg

66. Chickpea Cauliflower Tikka Masala

Preparation time: 15 minutes Cooking time: 40 minutes Servings: 6

Ingredients:
- 2 tablespoons olive oil
- 1 yellow onion, peeled and diced
- 4 garlic cloves, peeled and minced
- 1-inch piece fresh ginger, peeled and minced
- 2 tablespoons garam masala
- 1/4 teaspoon kosher or sea salt
- 1/2 teaspoon ground black pepper
- 1/4 teaspoon ground cayenne pepper
- 1/2 small head cauliflower, small florets
- 2 15-ounce cans of no-salt-added chickpeas, rinsed and drained
- 1 15-ounce can no-salt-added petite diced tomatoes, drained
- 1 1/2 cups unsalted vegetable broth
- 1/2 15-ounce can coconut milk
- Zest and juice of 1 lime
- 1/2 cup fresh cilantro leaves, chopped, divided
- 1 1/2 cups cooked fluffy brown rice, divided

Directions:
1. Warm up olive oil over medium heat, then put the onion and sauté for 4 to 5 minutes in a Dutch oven or stockpot. Stir in the garlic, ginger, garam masala, salt, black pepper, and cayenne pepper and toast for 30 to 60 seconds, until fragrant.
2. Stir in the cauliflower florets, chickpeas, diced tomatoes, and vegetable broth and increase to medium-high. Simmer for 15 minutes, until the cauliflower is fork-tender.
3. Remove, then stir in the coconut milk, lime juice, lime zest, and half of the cilantro. Taste and adjust the seasoning, if necessary. Serve over the rice and the remaining chopped cilantro.

Nutrition:
Calories: 323 Carbs: 4.4g Protein: 11g
Fat: 12g Sodium: 44 mg Potassium: 143.9mg

67. Eggplant Parmesan Stacks

Preparation time: 15 minutes Cooking time: 20 minutes Servings: 4

Ingredients:
- 1 large eggplant, cut into thick slices
- 2 tablespoons olive oil, divided
- 1/4 teaspoon kosher or sea salt
- 1/4 teaspoon ground black pepper
- 1 cup panko bread crumbs
- 1/4 cup freshly grated Parmesan cheese
- 5 to 6 garlic cloves, minced
- 1/2 pound fresh mozzarella, sliced
- 1 1/2 cups lower-sodium marinara
- 1/2 cup fresh basil leaves, torn

Directions:
1. Preheat the oven to 425F. Coat the eggplant slices in 1 tablespoon olive oil and sprinkle with the salt and black pepper. Put on a large baking sheet, then roast for 10 to 12 minutes, until soft with crispy edges. Remove the eggplant and set the oven to a low broil.
2. In a bowl, stir the remaining tablespoon of olive oil, bread crumbs, Parmesan cheese, and garlic. Remove the cooled eggplant from the baking sheet and clean it.
3. Create layers on the same baking sheet by stacking a roasted eggplant slice with a slice of mozzarella, a tablespoon of marinara, and a tablespoon of the bread crumb mixture, repeating with 2 layers of each ingredient. Process under the broiler for 3 to 4 minutes until the cheese is melted and bubbly.

Nutrition:
Calories: 377 Carbs: 2.9g Protein: 16g
Fat: 22g Sodium: 59mg Potassium: 118.6mg

68. Tomato and Olive Orecchiette with Basil Pesto

Preparation time: 15 minutes   Cooking time: 25 minutes   Servings: 6

Ingredients:
- 12 ounces orecchiette pasta
- 2 tablespoons olive oil
- 1-pint cherry tomatoes, quartered
- 1/2 cup basil pesto or store-bought pesto
- 1/4 cup kalamata olives, sliced
- 1 tablespoon dried oregano leaves
- 1/4 teaspoon kosher or sea salt
- 1/2 teaspoon freshly cracked black pepper
- 1/4 teaspoon crushed red pepper flakes
- 2 tablespoons freshly grated Parmesan cheese

Directions:
1. Boil a large pot of water. Cook the orecchiette, drain and transfer the pasta to a large nonstick skillet.
2. Put the skillet over medium-low heat, then heat the olive oil. Stir in the cherry tomatoes, pesto, olives, oregano, salt, black pepper, and crushed red pepper flakes. Cook for 8 to 10 minutes, until heated throughout. Serve the pasta with the freshly grated Parmesan cheese.

Nutrition:
Calories: 332   Carbs: 4.4g   Protein: 9g
Fat: 13g   Sodium: 389 mg   Potassium: 129.4mg

69. Italian Stuffed Portobello Mushroom Burgers

Preparation time: 15 minutes   Cooking time: 25 minutes   Servings: 4

Ingredients:
- 1 tablespoon olive oil
- 4 large portobello mushrooms, washed and dried
- 1/2 yellow onion, peeled and diced
- 4 garlic cloves, peeled and minced
- 1 can cannellini beans, drained
- 1/2 cup fresh basil leaves, torn
- 1/2 cup panko bread crumbs
- 1/2 teaspoon kosher or sea salt
- 1/4 teaspoon ground black pepper
- 1 cup lower-sodium marinara, divided
- 1/2 cup shredded mozzarella cheese
- 4 whole-wheat buns, toasted
- 1 cup fresh arugula

Directions:
1. Warmth up the olive oil in a large skillet to medium-high heat. Sear the mushrooms for 4 to 5 minutes per side, until slightly soft. Place on a baking sheet. Preheat the oven to a low broil.
2. Put the onion in the skillet and cook for 4 to 5 minutes, until slightly soft. Mix in the garlic then cook for 30 to 60 seconds. Move the onions plus garlic to a bowl. Add the cannellini beans and smash with the back of a fork to form a chunky paste. Stir in the basil, bread crumbs, salt, and black pepper and half of the marinara. Cook for 5 minutes.
3. Remove the bean mixture from the stove and divide among the mushroom caps. Spoon the remaining marinara over the stuffed mushrooms and top each with the mozzarella cheese. Simmer for 4 minutes, until the cheese is melted and bubbly. Transfer the burgers to the toasted whole wheat buns and top with the arugula.

Nutrition:
Calories: 407   Carbs: 6.3g   Protein: 25g
Fat: 9g   Sodium: 75mg   Potassium: 122.9mg

70. French Toast Sticks with Yogurt-Berry Dipping Sauce

Preparation time: 10 minutes   Cooking time: 10 minutes   Servings: 4

Ingredients:
For the French toast sticks
- 1 large egg
- 1 cup unsweetened almond milk
- 3 tablespoons ground cinnamon
- 1 tablespoon coconut sugar

- 4 slices whole-grain bread, each cut into 4 "sticks"

For the sauce
- 1 cup blueberries
- 1 tablespoon water
- 2 cups low-fat Greek yogurt

Directions:

To make the French toast sticks
1. Preheat the air fryer to 350F.
2. In a medium bowl, set together the egg, almond milk, cinnamon, and coconut sugar.
3. Dip each piece of bread into the egg mixture, dredging it on all sides and making sure it is fully soaked.
4. Cooking in batches if necessary, place the pieces of bread in the air fryer basket in a single layer and process for 5 minutes. Flip the sticks over and cook for another 3 minutes, or until golden brown.

To make the sauce
1. Meanwhile, in a saucepan over medium-high heat, merge the blueberries and water and cook, stirring occasionally, for 4 minutes, or until the berries start to burst and release their juices. While still warm, pour the blueberries over the Greek yogurt and gently stir to combine.
2. To serve, dip the French toast sticks in the yogurt-berry sauce while warm.

Nutrition:
Calories: 195
Fat: 10g
Protein: 8g
Carbs: 19g
Sodium: 87 mg
Potassium: 112mg

Dash Diet Cookbook

Chapter 5. Dinner

71. Apple Pie Crackers

Preparation time: 10 minutes   Cooking time: 120 minutes   Servings: 10 crackers
Ingredients:
- 2 tbsp. + 2 tsp. avocado oil
- 1 medium Granny Smith apple, roughly chopped
- 1/4 cup Erythritol
- 1/4 cup sunflower seeds, ground
- 1 3/4 cups flax seeds, roughly ground
- 1/8 tsp. cloves, ground
- 1/8 tsp. cardamom, ground
- 3 tbsp. nutmeg
- 1/4 tsp. ginger, ground

Directions:
1. Preheat your oven to 225F.
2. Set 2 baking sheets with parchment paper and keep them on the side.
3. Add oil, apple, Erythritol to a bowl and mix.
4. Transfer to a food processor and add remaining ingredients, process until combined.
5. Transfer batter to baking sheets, spread evenly, and cut into crackers.
6. Bake for 1 hour, flip and bake for another hour.
7. Let them cool and serve.
8. Enjoy!

Nutrition:
Calories: 70   Fat: 0g   Sodium: 6 mg
Carbs: 1/5g   Protein: 2g   Potassium: 121.6mg

72. Orange and Chili Garlic Sauce

Preparation time: 15 minutes   Cooking time: 8 hours   Servings: 5
Ingredients:
- 1/2 cup apple cider vinegar
- 4 lb. red jalapeno peppers, stems, seeds, and ribs removed, chopped
- 10 garlic cloves, chopped
- 1/2 cup tomato paste
- Juice of 1 orange zest
- 1/2 cup honey
- 2 tbsp. soy sauce
- 1/4 tsp. salt

Directions:
1. Add vinegar, garlic, peppers, tomato paste, orange juice, honey, zest, soy sauce, and salt to your Slow Cooker.
2. Stir and close the lid.
3. Cook on LOW for 8 hours.
4. Use as needed!

Nutrition:
Calories: 269   Fat: 9.7 g   Sodium: 53 mg
Carbs: 1.7 g   Protein: 25.6 g   Potassium: 112.2mg

73. Tantalizing Mushroom Gravy

Preparation time: 5 minutes   Cooking time: 5-8 hours   Servings: 2
Ingredients:
- 1 cup button mushrooms, sliced
- 3/4 cup low-fat buttermilk
- 1/3 cup water
- 1 medium onion, finely diced
- 2 garlic cloves, minced
- 2 tbsp. extra virgin olive oil
- 2 tbsp. all-purpose flour
- 1 tbsp. fresh rosemary, minced

- Freshly ground black pepper

Directions:
1. Add the listed ingredients to your Slow Cooker.
2. Place the lid and cook on LOW for 5-8 hours.
3. Serve warm and use as needed!

Nutrition:
Calories: 54　　　　　　　　Carbs: 4 g　　　　　　　　Sodium: 6 mg
Fat: 4 g;　　　　　　　　　Protein: 2 g　　　　　　　Potassium: 122.5mg

74. Everyday Vegetable Stock

Preparation time: 5 minutes　　Cooking time: 8-12 hours　　Servings: 10

Ingredients:
- 2 celery stalks (with leaves), quartered
- 4 oz. mushrooms, with stems
- 2 carrots, unpeeled and quartered
- 1 onion, unpeeled, quartered from pole to pole
- 1 garlic head, unpeeled, halved across the middle
- 2 fresh thyme sprigs
- 10 peppercorns
- 1/4 tsp. salt
- Enough water to fill 3 quarters of Slow Cooker

Directions:
1. Add celery, mushrooms, onion, carrots, garlic, thyme, salt, peppercorn, and water to your Slow Cooker.
2. Stir and cover.
3. Cook on LOW for 8-12 hours.
4. Strain the stock through a fine-mesh cloth/metal mesh and discard solids.
5. Use as needed.

Nutrition:
Calories: 38　　　　　　　　Carbs: 1 g　　　　　　　　Sodium: 24 mg
Fat: 5 g　　　　　　　　　Protein: 0 g　　　　　　　Potassium: 112.2mg

75. Grilled Chicken with Lemon and Fennel

Preparation time: 5 minutes　　Cooking time: 25 minutes　　Servings: 4

Ingredients:
- 2 cups chicken fillets, cut and skewed
- 1 large fennel bulb
- 2 garlic cloves
- 1 jar green olives
- 1 lemon

Directions:
1. Preheat your grill to medium-high.
2. Crush garlic cloves.
3. Take a bowl and add olive oil, and season with sunflower seeds and pepper.
4. Coat chicken skewers with the marinade.
5. Transfer them under the grill and grill for 20 minutes, making sure to turn them halfway through until golden.
6. Zest half of the lemon and cut the other half into quarters.
7. Cut the fennel bulb into similarly sized segments.
8. Brush olive oil all over the garlic clove segments and cook for 3-5 minutes.
9. Chop them and add them to the bowl with the marinade.
10. Add lemon zest and olives.
11. Once the meat is ready, serve with the vegetable mix.
12. Enjoy!

Nutrition:
Calories: 88　　　　　　　　　　　Fat: 9 g　　　　　　　　　　　　Sodium: 74 mg
Carbs: 1 g　　　　　　　　　　　　Protein: 1 g　　　　　　　　　　Potassium: 112.5mg

76. Black Eyed Peas and Spinach Platter

Preparation time: 10 minutes　　　Cooking time: 8 hours　　　　　Servings: 4

Ingredients:
- 1 cup black-eyed peas, soaked overnight, and drained
- 2 cups low-sodium vegetable broth
- 1 can (15 oz.) tomatoes, diced with juice
- 8 oz. ham, chopped
- 1 onion, chopped
- 2 garlic cloves, minced
- 1 tsp. oregano, dried
- 1/4 tsp. salt
- 1/2 tsp. black pepper, freshly ground
- 1/2 tsp. mustard, ground
- 1 bay leaf

Directions:
1. Add the listed ingredients to your Slow Cooker and stir.
2. Place lid and cook on LOW for 8 hours.
3. Discard the bay leaf.
4. Serve and enjoy!

Nutrition:
Calories: 159　　　　　　　　　　　Fat: 3.9 g
Protein: 3 g　　　　　　　　　　　 Sodium: 6 mg
Carbs: 2.4 g　　　　　　　　　　　 Potassium: 132mg

77. Humble Mushroom Rice

Preparation time: 10 minutes　　　Cooking time: 3 hours　　　　　Servings: 3

Ingredients:
- 1/2 cup rice
- 2 green onions chopped
- 1 garlic clove, minced
- 1/4 lb. baby Portobello mushrooms, sliced
- 1 cup vegetable stock

Directions:
1. Add rice, onions, garlic, mushrooms, and stock to your Slow Cooker.
2. Stir well and place the lid.
3. Cook on LOW for 3 hours.
4. Stir and divide amongst serving platters.
5. Enjoy!

Nutrition:
Calories: 359　　　　　　　　　　　Fat: 7 g　　　　　　　　　　　　Protein: 14 g
Carbs: 6.1 g　　　　　　　　　　　 Sodium: 19 mg　　　　　　　　　Potassium: 125.3mg

78. Roasted Root Vegetables with Goat's Cheese Polenta

Preparation time: 35 minutes　　　Cooking time: 25 hours　　　　Servings: 2

Ingredients:
Polenta:
- 2 cups low-sodium vegetable/chicken broth
- 1/2 cup polenta fine cornmeal/corn grits
- 1/4 cup goat's cheese
- 1 tbsp. extra-virgin olive oil or butter
- 1/4 tsp. kosher salt
- 1/4 tsp. ground pepper

Vegetables:
- 1 tbsp. extra-virgin olive oil or butter
- 1 clove garlic, smashed
- 2 cups roasted root vegetables
- 1 tbsp. torn fresh sage
- 2 tsp. prepared pesto
- Fresh parsley for garnish

Directions:
1. To prepare the polenta: Bring the broth to a boil in a medium saucepan. Set the heat to low and gradually add the polenta whisking vigorously to avoid clumping. Secure and process for 10 minutes. Stir, secure, and continue cooking until thickened and creamy. Stir in the goat's cheese, oil (or butter), salt, and pepper.
2. Meanwhile, to prepare the vegetables: Heat the oil (or butter) in a medium skillet over medium heat. Attach the garlic and cook, stirring, until fragrant, about 1 minute. Add the roasted vegetables and cook, stirring often, until heated through, 2 to 4 minutes. Stir in the torn sage and cook until fragrant, about 1 minute more. Serving Suggestion: Serve the vegetables over the polenta, topped with pesto. Garnish with parsley, if desired.

Nutrition:
Calories: 150　　Fat: 8 g　　Sodium: 120 mg
Carbs: 24 g　　Protein: 1 g　　Potassium: 129.4mg

79. Fish Stew

Preparation time: 10 minutes　　Cooking time: 30 minutes　　Servings: 4

Ingredients:
- 1 red onion, sliced
- 2 tbsp. olive oil
- 1-lb. white fish fillets, boneless, skinless, and cubed
- 1 avocado, pitted and chopped
- 1 tbsp. oregano, chopped
- 1 cup chicken stock
- 2 tomatoes, cubed
- 1 tsp. sweet paprika
- A pinch of salt and black pepper
- 1 tbsp. parsley, chopped
- Juice of 1 lime

Directions:
1. Warm-up oil in a pot over medium heat, add the onion, and sauté within 5 minutes.
2. Add the fish, the avocado, and the other ingredients, toss, cook over medium heat for 25 minutes more, divide into bowls and serve for dinner.

Nutrition:
Calories: 78　　Fat: 1 g　　Sodium: 51 mg
Carbs: 8 g　　Protein: 11 g　　Potassium: 121.4mg

80. Gnocchi Pomodoro

Preparation Time: 35 minutes　　Cooking Time: 35 minutes　　Servings: 4

Ingredients
- 3 tbsp. extra-virgin olive oil, divided
- 1 medium onion, finely chopped
- 2 large cloves garlic, minced
- 1/4 tsp. crushed red pepper
- 1 1/2 cups no-salt-added whole tomatoes, pulsed in a food processor until chunky
- 1/4 tsp. salt
- 1 tbsp. butter
- 1/4 cup chopped fresh basil
- 1 (17.5 oz.) package shelf-stable gnocchi or (12 oz.) package frozen cauliflower gnocchi
- Grated parmesan cheese, for garnish

Directions:
1. Heat 2 tbsp. of the oil in a skillet. Set the onion and cook, stirring, until softened, for about 5 minutes.
2. Attach the garlic and crushed red pepper and cook until softened for about 1 minute.

3. Attach the tomatoes and salt and set to a simmer. Lower the heat to maintain the boil and cook, stirring often, until thickened (about 20 minutes).
4. Detach from the heat and stir in the butter and basil.
5. Meanwhile, heat the remaining 1 tbsp. of oil in a non-stick skillet. Attach the gnocchi and cook, stirring often, until plumped and starting to brown (5 to 7 minutes). Set the gnocchi to the tomato sauce and stir until coated.

Nutrition:
Calories: 448
Protein: 10.1g
Carbs: 6.4g
Fat: 14.2g
Sodium: 66.6mg
Potassium: 142mg

81. Slow-Cooked Pasta e Fagioli Soup

Preparation time: 8 hours 15 minutes
Cooking Time: 15 minutes
Servings: 6

Ingredients
- 2 cups chopped onions
- 1 cup chopped carrots
- 1 cup chopped celery
- 1 lb. pre-cooked chicken thighs, diced
- 4 cups cooked whole-wheat rotini pasta
- 6 cups reduced-sodium chicken broth
- 4 tsp. dried Italian seasoning
- 1/4 tsp. salt
- 15 oz. /1 can no-salt-added white beans, rinsed
- 4 cups baby spinach
- 4 tbsp. chopped fresh basil, divided (optional)
- 2 tbsp. best-quality extra-virgin olive oil
- 1/2 cup grated Parmigiano-Reggiano cheese

Directions:
1. Set the onions, carrots, and celery in a large sealable plastic bag.
2. Place the cooled, cooked chicken and cooked pasta in another bag.
3. Secure both bags and freeze for up to 5 days. Defrost the bags in the refrigerator overnight before processing.
4. Bring the vegetable mixture to a large slow cooker. Add the broth, Italian seasoning, and salt. Cover and cook on low for 71/4 hours.
5. Add the beans, spinach, 2 tbsp. of the basil, if using, and the defrosted chicken and pasta. Cook for 45 minutes more. Ladle the soup into bowls.

Nutrition:
Calories: 457
Protein: 33.9g
Carbohydrates: 2.3g
Fat: 18.3g
Sodium: 53mg
Potassium: 154mg

82. Salmon Couscous Salad

Preparation time: 10 minutes
Cooking time: 10 minutes
Servings: 1

Ingredients
- 1/4 cup sliced cremini mushrooms
- 1/4 cup diced eggplant
- 3 cups baby spinach
- 2 tbsp. white-wine vinaigrette, divided
- 1/4 cup cooked Israeli couscous, preferably whole-wheat
- 4 oz. cooked salmon
- 1/4 cup sliced dried apricots
- 2 tbsp. crumbled goat's cheese (1/2 oz.)

Directions:
1. Glaze a small skillet with cooking spray and warmth over medium-high heat. Add the mushrooms and eggplant. Cook, stirring, until lightly browned and the juices have been released (3 to 5 minutes). Remove from the heat and set aside.
2. Toss the spinach with 1 tbsp. plus 1 tsp. of vinaigrette and place on a 9-inch plate.

Dash Diet Cookbook

Nutrition:
Calories: 464   Carbs: 4.7g   Sodium: 52.1mg
Protein: 34.8g   Fat: 22.1g   Potassium: 198mg

83. Roasted Salmon with Smoky Chickpeas and Greens

Preparation time: 40 minutes   Cooking time: 40 minutes   Servings: 4

Ingredients

- 2 tbsp. extra-virgin olive oil, divided
- 1 tbsp. smoked paprika
- 1/4 tsp. salt, divided, plus a pinch
- 1 (15 oz.) can no-salt-added chickpeas, rinsed
- 1/3 cup buttermilk
- 1/4 cup mayonnaise
- 1/4 cup chopped fresh chives and/or dill, plus more for garnish
- 1/2 tsp. ground pepper, divided
- 1/4 tsp. garlic powder
- 10 cups chopped kale
- 1/4 cup water
- 1 1/4 lbs. wild salmon, cut into 4 portions

Directions:
1. Position racks in the upper third and middle of the oven. Preheat to 425F.
2. Combine 1 tbsp. of the oil, the paprika, and 1/4 tsp. of salt in a medium bowl.
3. Very thoroughly pat the chickpeas dry, then toss with the paprika mixture.
4. Spread the chickpea mixture in a baking sheet. Bake the chickpeas on the upper rack, stirring twice, for 30 minutes.
5. Meanwhile, merge the buttermilk, mayonnaise, herbs, 1/4 tsp. of pepper, and garlic powder in a blender until smooth. Set aside.
6. Heat the remaining 1 tbsp. of oil in a skillet. Attach the kale and cook, stirring occasionally, for 2 minutes.
7. Attach the water and continue cooking until the kale is tender, about 5 minutes more. Remove from the heat and stir in a pinch of salt.
8. Detach the chickpeas from the oven and push them to one side of the pan. Set the salmon on the other side and season with the remaining 1/4 tsp. each of salt and pepper. Process until the salmon is just cooked through, 5 to 8 minutes.

Nutrition:
Calories: 447   Carbs: 3g   Sodium: 67mg
Protein: 37g   Fat: 21.8g   Potassium: 187mg

84. Salmon with Salsa

Preparation time: 10 minutes   Cooking time: 8 minutes   Servings: 1

Ingredients:
For Salsa:

- 1/4 cup red bell pepper, seedless and chopped
- 1 tablespoon red onion, chopped

For Salmon:

- 1/2 tablespoon extra-virgin olive oil
- 1 tablespoon fresh cilantro leaves, chopped
- 1/2 cup fresh pineapple chopped
- 1/2 tablespoon fresh lemon juice
- Fresh ground black pepper to taste
- 1 Salmon fillets
- 1/4 of salt
- Fresh ground black pepper to taste

Directions:
For Salsa:
1. Set a bowl and merge all the ingredients together.
2. Refrigerate before serving.

For Salmon:
1. First, season salmon with salt and black pepper.

2. In a large frying pan, warmth the oil over medium-high heat.
3. Add Salmon, skins side up and cook for about four minutes.
4. Carefully change the side of fillets and cook for about four minutes more.
5. Divide salsa onto both plates alongside salmon fillets and serve.
6. Enjoy!

Nutrition:
Calories: 338 Carbohydrates: 10.4g Sodium: 6 mg
Fat: 18.2g Protein: 35.5g Potassium: 143mg

85. Bruschetta Chicken

Preparation time: 8 minutes Cooking time: 12 minutes Servings: 2

Ingredients:
For Chicken:
- 1 chicken boneless, skinless chicken breasts, halved horizontally
- 1 1/2 teaspoon salt-free Italian seasoning
- 1/2 tablespoon olive oil
- 1 teaspoon garlic, minced

For Topping:
- 1 1/2 garlic cloves, chopped finely
- 2 Roma tomatoes, chopped finely
- 2 tablespoons fresh basil, shredded
- 1 tablespoon olive oil

Directions:
For Chicken:
1. Take a bowl, add the chicken, garlic and Italian seasoning and mix them well altogether.
2. Take a frying pan and heat the oil over medium-high heat and brown the chicken breasts for about 6 minutes per side.

Topping:
1. Take a bowl, merge all the ingredients except the Parmesan cheese and mix.
2. Remove the frying-pan from the heat and divide the chicken breasts onto serving plates.
3. Serve immediately.

Nutrition:
Calories: 234 Carbs: 5.9g Sodium: 19 mg
Fat: 13.7g Protein: 22.9g Potassium: 176mg

86. Quinoa Power Salad

Preparation time: 40 minutes Cooking time: 20 minutes Servings: 2

Ingredients
- 1 medium sweet potato, skinned and cut into 1/2-inch thick wedges
- 1/2 red onion, cut into 1/4-inch thick wedges
- 2 tbsp. extra-virgin olive oil, divided
- 1/2 tsp. garlic powder
- 1/4 tsp. salt
- 8 oz. chicken tender
- 2 tbsp. whole-grain mustard
- 1 tbsp. finely sliced shallot
- 1 tablespoon pure maple syrup
- 1 tbsp. cider vinegar
- 4 cups greens/kale spinach or arugula, washed and dried
- 1/2 cup cooked red quinoa, cooled
- 1 tbsp. unsalted sunflower seeds, toasted

Directions:
1. Preheat the oven to 425F. Set the sweet potato and onion with 1 tbsp. of oil, the garlic powder, and 1/8 tsp. of salt in a medium bowl.
2. Scatter the mixture on a large rimmed baking sheet and roast for 15 minutes.
3. Meanwhile, add the chicken and 1 tbsp. of the mustard to a bowl. Toss to coat the chicken.
4. When the vegetables have crisp for 15 minutes, remove them from the oven and stir. Add the chicken to the chicken on the baking sheet. Set to the oven and continue roasting until the vegetables

start to brown and the chicken is cooked through (about 10 minutes more). Remove from the oven and let cool.
   5. Meanwhile, whisk the shallot, maple syrup, vinegar, and the remaining oil, mustard, and salt in a large bowl.

Nutrition:
Calories: 466　　　　　　　　　Carbs: 5.4g　　　　　　　　　Sodium: 16.2mg
Protein: 28.7g　　　　　　　　 Fat: 21.1g　　　　　　　　　 Potassium: 112mg

87. Balsamic Roast Chicken Breast

Preparation time: 10 minutes　　　Cooking time: 35 minutes　　　Servings: 2

Ingredients:
- 2, 4 ounces skinless chicken breasts
- black pepper to taste
- 1 teaspoon finely chopped fresh garlic
- 1 tablespoon fresh thyme chopped
- 1 teaspoon grape seed oil
- 1/2 cup Balsamic vinegar, plus 2 tbsp. extra
- 8 ounces broccoli florets
- 2 teaspoons Balsamic vinegar
- 2 teaspoons grapeseed oil
- Black pepper to taste
- 2 tablespoons toasted cashew nuts
- Sprigs of fresh parsley to garnish

Directions:
1. Place the 1/2 cup Balsamic vinegar, garlic, pepper, thyme and oil in a small pot and bring to a boil. 2. Simmer for about 3 minutes or until the liquid has reduced by about half. Cool this mixture in the freezer for 5 minutes.
2. Oil a baking tray and set the chicken on it. Cover the chicken in the cooled marinade and leave to chill for 30 minutes.
3. Meanwhile, preheat the oven to 375F. Mix the broccoli florets with two teaspoons of Balsamic vinegar, two teaspoons of grape seed oil, and pepper.
4. Oil a second baking tray and lay the veg out on it. After 30 minutes, cover the marinated chicken with foil and place in the oven to roast for 30-35 minutes.
5. For the last 15-20 minutes, place the broccoli in the oven to roast too. Give them a good stir at least once while cooking.
6. Once the chicken is cooked, serve it hot with the broccoli on the side.

Nutrition:
Calories: 304　　　　　　　　　Sodium: 56mg　　　　　　　　Protein: 28g
Fat: 12g　　　　　　　　　　　Carbs: 3g　　　　　　　　　　Potassium: 187mg

88. Stuffed Eggplant Shells

Preparation time: 15 minutes　　　Cooking time: 25 minutes　　　Servings: 2

Ingredients:
- 1 medium eggplant
- 1 cup water
- 1 tablespoon olive oil
- 4 ounces cooked white beans
- 1/4 cup onion, chopped
- 1/2 cup red, green, or yellow bell peppers, chopped
- 1 cup canned unsalted tomatoes
- 1/4 cup tomato liquid
- 1/4 cup celery, chopped
- 1 cup fresh mushrooms, sliced
- 3/4 cup whole-wheat breadcrumbs
- Black pepper, to taste

Directions:
1. Preheat the oven to 350F.
2. Set a baking dish with cooking spray and set it aside.
3. Trim and cut the eggplant in half, lengthwise.
4. Set out the pulp using a spoon and leave the shell about 1/4-inch thick.

5. Place the shells in the baking dish with their cut side up.
6. Attach water to the bottom of the dish.
7. Dice the eggplant pulp into cubes and set them aside.
8. Add oil to an iron skillet and heat it over medium heat.
9. Stir in the onions, peppers, chopped eggplant pulp, tomatoes, celery, mushrooms, and tomato juice.
10. Cook for 10 minutes on simmering heat, then stir in the beans, black pepper, and breadcrumbs.
11. Divide this mixture into the eggplant shells.
12. Cover the shells with a foil sheet and bake for 15 minutes.
13. Serve warm.

Nutrition:
Calories: 305　　　　Sodium: 82mg　　　　Protein: 15.2g
Fat: 12.7g　　　　　Carbs: 6g　　　　　　Potassium: 132mg

89. Zucchini Pepper Kebabs

Preparation time: 15 minutes　　Cooking time: 40 minutes　　Servings: 4

Ingredients:
- 1 small zucchini, sliced into 8 pieces
- 1 red onion, cut into 4 wedges
- 1 green bell pepper, cut into 4 chunks
- 8 cherry tomatoes
- 8 button mushrooms
- 1 red bell pepper, cut into 4 chunks
- 1/2 cup fat-free Italian dressing,
- 1/2 cup brown rice
- 1 cup water

Directions:
1. Toss the tomatoes with the zucchini, onion, peppers, and mushrooms in a bowl.
2. Stir in the Italian dressing and mix well to coat the vegetables.
3. Marinate the mixture for 10 minutes.
4. Bring the water with the rice to a boil in a saucepan, then reduce the heat to a simmer. 5. Cover the rice and cook for 30 minutes until the rice is done.
5. Meanwhile, preheat the broiler on medium heat.
6. Grease the broiler rack with cooking spray and place it 4 inches below the heat source. 8. Put 2 mushrooms, 2 tomatoes, 2 zucchini slices, 1 onion wedge, 1 green pepper slice, and 1 red pepper slice onto a skewer (4 skewers in total).
7. Grill the kebabs per side.
8. Serve warm.

Nutrition:
Calories: 376　　　　Sodium: 76mg　　　　Protein: 10g
Fat: 11g　　　　　　Carbs: 6.7g　　　　　Potassium: 198mg

90. Corn Stuffed Peppers

Preparation time: 15 minutes　　Cooking time: 25 minutes　　Servings: 4

Ingredients:
- 4 red or green bell peppers
- 1 tablespoon olive oil
- 1/4 cup onion, chopped
- 1 green bell pepper, chopped
- 2 1/2 cups fresh corn kernels
- 1/8 teaspoon chili powder
- 2 tablespoons parsley, chopped
- 3 egg whites
- 1/2 cup skim milk
- 1/2 cup water

Directions:
1. Preheat the oven to 350F.
2. Grease a baking dish with cooking spray.
3. Cut the bell peppers from the top and remove their seeds.
4. Place the peppers in the baking dish with their cut side up.

5. Add the oil to a skillet, then heat it on medium flame.
6. Stir in the onion, corn, and chopped green pepper. Sauté for 5 minutes. 7. Add the cilantro and chili powder. Switch the heat to low.
7. Whisk the milk and egg whites in a bowl.
8. Pour this mixture into the skillet and cook for 5 minutes while stirring. 10. Divide this mixture into each pepper.
9. 11. Add some water to the baking dish.
10. Cover the stuffed peppers with an aluminum sheet.
11. Bake for 15 minutes, then serve warm.

Nutrition:
Calories: 361   Carbs: 2.8g   Protein: 9g
Fat: 16g   Sodium: 55mg   Potassium: 132mg

91. South Asian Baked salmon

Preparation time: 15 minutes   Cooking time: 20 minutes   Servings: 2

Ingredients:
- 1/2 cup sugar-free pineapple juice
- 2 garlic cloves, minced
- 1 teaspoon tamari
- 1/4 teaspoon ground ginger
- 2 salmon fillets
- 1/4 teaspoon sesame oil
- Ground black pepper, to taste
- 1 cup diced fresh fruit, as desired

Directions:
1. Mix the pineapple juice with the garlic, ginger, and tamari in a bowl.
2. Place the fish in a baking dish.
3. Pour the pineapple mixture over the fish and marinate in the refrigerator for 1 hour, gently flipping the fish halfway through.
4. Meanwhile, preheat the oven to 375°F.
5. Spread out two squares of aluminum foil and layer them with cooking spray.
6. Place the salmon fillets on each square.
7. Top the fish with the sesame oil, pepper, and diced fruit.
8. Fold the aluminum sheets to seal the fish and place them on a baking sheet.
9. Bake for 20 minutes, turning the parcels halfway through.
10. Serve warm.

Nutrition:
Calories: 245   Sodium: 131mg   Protein: 23g
Fat: 16g   Carbs: 2g   Potassium: 112mg

92. Sweet Potato Carbonara with Spinach and Mushrooms

Preparation time: 40 minutes   Cooking time: 20 minutes   Servings: 5

Ingredients:
- 2 lbs. sweet potatoes, peeled
- 3 large eggs, beaten
- 1 cup grated parmesan cheese
- 1/4 tsp. salt
- 1/4 tsp. ground pepper
- 1 tbsp. extra-virgin olive oil
- 3 strips center-cut bacon, chopped
- 8 oz. sliced mushrooms
- 2 cloves garlic, minced
- 5 oz. baby spinach

Directions:
1. Process a pot of water on to boil.
2. Cut the sweet potatoes lengthwise into long, thin strands using a spiral vegetable slicer or julienne vegetable peeler.

3. Process the sweet potatoes in the boiling water, gently stirring once or twice, until just starting to soften but not completely crisp (around 1 1/2 to 3 minutes). Set aside 1/4 cup of the cooking water, then drain. Set back the noodles to the pot, off the heat.
4. Merge the eggs, parmesan, salt, pepper, and the reserved water in a bowl. Spill the mixture over the noodles and gently toss with tongs until evenly coated.
5. Heat the oil in a large skillet over medium heat. Attach the bacon and mushrooms and cook, stirring often, until the liquid has evaporated and the mushrooms are starting to brown (around 6 to 8 minutes).
6. Add the garlic and cook, stirring, until fragrant, for about 1 minute. Attach the spinach and cook, stirring, until wilted, for 1 to 2 minutes. Attach the vegetables to the noodles and toss to merge.

Nutrition:
Calories: 312 Carbs: 3.6g Sodium: 586.6mg
Protein: 14.5g Fat: 12.2g Potassium: 112.6mg

93. Hazelnut-Parsley Roast Tilapia

Preparation time: 30 minutes Cooking time: 20 minutes Servings: 4

Ingredients:
- 2 tbsp. olive oil, divided
- 4 (5 oz.) tilapia fillets (fresh or frozen, thawed)
- 1/3 cup finely chopped hazelnuts
- 1/4 cup finely chopped fresh parsley
- 1 small shallot, minced
- 2 tsp. lemon zest
- 1/8 tsp. salt plus 1/4 tsp., divided
- 1/4 tsp. ground pepper, divided
- 1 1/2 tbsp. lemon juice

Directions:
1. Preheat the oven to 450F. Set a large rimmed baking sheet with foil and brush with 1 tbsp. of oil.
2. Bring the fish to room temperature by leaving it on the counter for 15 minutes.
3. Meanwhile, stir together the hazelnuts, parsley, shallot, lemon zest, 1 tsp. of oil, 1/8 tsp. salt, and 1/8 tsp. pepper in a small bowl.
4. Set both sides of the fish dry with a paper towel. Bring the fish on the prepared baking sheet. Garnish both sides of the fish with lemon juice and the remaining 2 tsp. of oil. Flavor both sides of the fish evenly with the remaining 1/4 tsp. salt and 1/8 tsp. pepper.
5. Set the hazelnut mixture evenly among the tops of the fillets and pat gently to adhere.
6. Crisp the fish until it is opaque, firm, and just beginning to flake (7 to 10 minutes).

Nutrition:
Calories: 262 Carbs: 3.3g Sodium: 94.7mg
Protein: 30.2g Fat: 15g Potassium: 132mg

94. Fig and Goat's Cheese Salad

Preparation time: 10 minutes Cooking time: 10 minutes Servings: 1

Ingredients:
- 2 cups mixed salad greens
- 4 dried figs, stemmed and sliced
- 1 oz. fresh goat's cheese, crumbled
- 1 1/2 tbsp. slivered almonds, preferably toasted
- 2 tsp. extra-virgin olive oil
- 2 tsp. balsamic vinegar
- 1/2 tsp. honey
- 1/4 tsp. of salt
- Freshly ground pepper to taste

Directions:
1. Combine the greens, figs, goat's cheese, and almonds in a medium bowl.
2. Stir together the oil, vinegar, honey, salt, and pepper.

Nutrition:
Calories: 340 Carbs: 3.8g Sodium: 39.5mg
Protein: 10.4g Fat: 21g Potassium: 152mg

95. Masala Chickpeas

Preparation time: 10 minutes Cooking time: 25 minutes Servings: 4

Ingredients:
- 1 1/2 teaspoon garam masala powder
- 1 teaspoon smoked paprika
- 1 teaspoon jeera powder
- 1 teaspoon ground coriander
- 1 teaspoon turmeric powder
- 1/4 teaspoon Cayenne pepper
- 1 tablespoon canola oil
- 1/2 teaspoon black mustard seeds
- 2 tablespoons jeera seeds 1 white onion, diced
- 4 tablespoons finely chopped garlic
- 1 large sweet red pepper, diced
- 2 rosa tomatoes, roughly chopped
- 1/2 cup broccoli florets
- 1 medium carrot, peeled and cut into cubes
- 2 cups water
- 30 ounces cooked chickpeas, rinsed and drained
- 1 tablespoon tomato paste
- 10 ounces frozen kale, thawed
- Black pepper to taste
- 2 tbsp. finely chopped fresh coriander, plus extra to garnish

Directions:
1. In a small bowl, make the spice blend by mixing all the dried spices, except for the jeera seeds and mustard seeds. Set aside.
2. Warmth the oil in a medium pot, then add in the mustard seeds and jeera seeds.
3. Process for 10 seconds before adding in the onion and garlic. Fry for 3 minutes.
4. Add in the following vegetables: red pepper, tomatoes, broccoli, and carrots. Then cook the mixture on medium heat for about 6 minutes.
5. Pour in two cups of water, then add the chickpeas, tomato paste, kale, and black pepper to taste.
6. Set to a slow boil and cook for about 15-20 minutes, or until the vegetables are cooked through and the stew smells aromatic.
7. Enjoy.

Nutrition:
Calories: 309 Sodium: 34mg Protein: 15g
Fat: 7g Carbs: 5g Potassium: 132mg

96. Orecchiette with Broccoli Rabe

Preparation time: 30 minutes Cooking time: 15 minutes Servings: 6

Ingredients:
- 1/4 tsp. salt
- 12 oz. orecchiette pasta (about 31/2 cups)
- 2 lbs. broccoli rabe (about 2 bunches)
- 1/4 cup extra-virgin olive oil
- 3 cloves garlic, chopped
- 1/2 tsp. crushed red pepper
- 8 anchovy fillets, chopped
- 1 pint cherry tomatoes, halved

Directions:
1. Set 2 quarts of water to boil in a large pot. Stir in salt, add the pasta, and cook until just tender. Drain, set aside 1/2 cup of the water.
2. Meanwhile, thoroughly wash the broccoli rabe and trim off the tough ends. Chop the rabe into 2-inch lengths. Leave some water clinging to the leaves and stems (this will help create a sauce).
3. Heat the oil in a large skillet over medium heat until it starts to shimmer. Add the garlic, crushed red pepper, and anchovies, pressing the fillets until they dissolve.
4. Attach the broccoli rabe. Cook, stirring, until almost tender (6 to 10 minutes).
5. Set the tomatoes and toss until they begin to soften (about 2 minutes).
6. Attach the pasta and toss to coat. If it's too dry, attach a little of the reserved pasta water.

Nutrition:
Calories: 359
Protein: 14.9g
Carbs: 4.5g
Fat: 12.1g
Sodium: 88.5mg
Potassium: 139mg

97. Chicken and Strawberry Salad

Preparation time: 10 minutes **Cooking time:** 16 minutes **Servings:** 4

Ingredients:
- 4 tablespoons olive oil
- 1 tablespoon Erythritol
- 2 cups fresh strawberries
- 1 pound boneless, skinless chicken breasts
- 4 tablespoons lemon juice
- 1/2 garlic clove, minced
- 4 cups fresh spinach, torn
- 1/4tsp. of salt
- Fresh ground black pepper to taste

Directions:
1. For marinade: Take a bowl and add oil, lemon juice, Erythritol, garlic, salt and black pepper and beat them well until well combined.
2. In a large resalable plastic bag place chicken and 3/4 cup marinade.
3. Secure the bag and shake it to coat well. Refrigerate overnight.
4. Cover the bowl of remaining marinade and refrigerate before serving.
5. Preheat the grill to medium heat.
6. Grease the grill grate finely.
7. Detach the chicken from bag and discard the marinade.
8. Place the chicken onto grill grate and grill it covered for about five to eight minutes per side. 9. Remove chicken from grill and cut into small pieces.
9. Take a large bowl, add the chicken pieces, strawberries and spinach and mix everything together. 11. Place the reserved marinade and toss to coat well.
10. Serve immediately and enjoy!

Nutrition:
Calories: 370
Fat: 22.9g
Carbs: 1.8g
Protein: 34.3g
Sodium: 6 mg
Potassium: 179.8mg

98. Mixed Vegetable Salad with Lime Dressing

Preparation time: 30 minutes **Cooking time:** 30 minutes **Servings:** 6

Ingredients:
- 1/4 cup canola oil
- 1/4 cup extra-virgin olive oil
- 3 tbsp. lime juice
- 11/2 tbsp. finely chopped fresh cilantro
- 1/4 tsp. salt
- 1/2 tsp. ground pepper
- 2 cups mixed vegetables, steamed (sliced small red potatoes, carrots or beets, green beans, peas) and raw (sliced radishes, cucumbers, or tomatoes)
- 6 leaves romaine or leaf lettuce
- 1 small bunch watercress, large stems removed
- 1 large hard-boiled egg, sliced
- 1 thick slice of red onion
- Crumbled Mexican queso fresco, feta, or farmer cheese for garnish

Directions:
1. Whisk the canola and olive oils, lime juice, cilantro, salt, and pepper in a medium bowl until thoroughly blended.
2. Attach the mixed vegetables and toss to coat.

Nutrition:
Calories: 214
Protein: 2.6g
Carbs: 7.7g
Fat: 19.8
Sodium: 16.6mg
Potassium: 232mg

99. Spinach Ginger Lentils

Preparation time: 10 minutes
Cooking time: 16 minutes
Servings: 4
Ingredients:

- 1 tablespoon olive oil
- 1 shallot, minced
- 1 teaspoon ground ginger
- 1/2 teaspoon curry powder
- 1/2 teaspoon ground turmeric
- 1 cup yellow lentils, drained
- 1 1/2 cups vegetable stock
- 1/2 cup light coconut milk
- 2 cups baby spinach leaves, chopped
- 1/4 teaspoon salt
- Garnish:
- 1 teaspoon white sesame seeds
- 1 tablespoon fresh cilantro, chopped

Directions:
1. Add the olive oil to a saucepan, then heat it over medium flame.
2. Stir in the ginger, shallot, turmeric, and curry powder.
3. Sauté for 1 minute, then add the stock, coconut milk, and lentils.
4. Let the lentils boil, then reduce the heat to a simmer.
5. Partially cover the pan, then cook for 12 minutes.
6. Meanwhile, toast the sesame seeds in a dry skillet until they turn brown.
7. Attach the spinach to the lentils and cook for 3 minutes.
8. Adjust the seasoning with salt.
9. Set with the toasted sesame seeds and cilantro.
10. Serve warm.

Nutrition:
Calories: 263
Fat: 7.5g
Carbs: 6g
Protein: 14g
Sodium: 5mg
Potassium: 232mg

100. Basil Halibut

Preparation time: 10 minutes
Cooking time: 20 minutes
Servings: 4
Ingredients:

- 4 halibut fillets, 4 ounces each
- 2 teaspoons olive oil
- 1 tablespoon garlic, minced
- 2 tomatoes, diced
- 2 Tablespoons basil, fresh and chopped
- 1 teaspoon oregano, fresh and chopped

Directions:
1. Heat the oven to 350F and then get out a 9 by 13-inch pan. Spray it down with cooking spray.
2. Toss the basil, olive oil, garlic, oregano, and tomato together in a bowl. Pour this over your fish in the pan.
3. Bake for twelve minutes. Your fish should be flakey.

Nutrition:
Calories: 128
Protein: 21g
Fat: 4g
Carbs: 3g
Sodium: 31mg
Potassium: 182mg

101. Leek and Cauliflower Soup

Preparation time: 20 minutes
Cooking time: 20 minutes
Servings: 6
Ingredients:

- 1 tablespoon olive oil
- 1 leek, trimmed and sliced thin
- 1 yellow onion, peeled and diced
- 1 head cauliflower, chopped into florets
- 3 cloves garlic, minced
- 2 tablespoons thyme, fresh and chopped

- 1 teaspoon smoked paprika
- 1/4 teaspoons sea salt, fine
- 1/4 teaspoon ground cayenne pepper
- 1 tablespoon heavy cream
- 3 cups vegetable stock, unsalted
- 1/2 lemon, juiced and zested

Directions:
1. Heat your oil in a stockpot over medium heat, and add in your leek, onion, and cauliflower. Process for 5 minutes until the onion begins to soften. Add in your garlic, thyme, smoked paprika, salt, pepper and cayenne. Pour in your vegetable stock and bring it to a simmer, cooking for fifteen minutes. Your cauliflower should be very tender.
2. Detach from heat and stir in your lemon juice, lemon zest and cream. Use an immersion blender to puree and serve warm.

Nutrition:
Calories: 92 Fat: 4g Sodium: 55mg
Protein: 5g Carbs: 3g Potassium: 142mg

102. Sweet and Sour Cabbage and Apples

Preparation time: 15 minutes Cooking time: 8 hours Servings: 4

Ingredients:
- 1/4 cup honey
- 1/4 cup apple cider vinegar
- 2 tablespoons orange chili-garlic sauce
- 1/4 teaspoon sea salt
- 3 sweet tart apples, peeled, cored and sliced
- 2 heads green cabbage, cored and shredded
- 1 sweet red onion, thinly sliced

Directions:
1. Take a small bowl and whisk in honey, orange-chili garlic sauce, and vinegar.
2. Stir well.
3. Add honey mix, apples, onion and cabbage to your Slow Cooker and stir.
4. Cook on low for 8 hours.
5. Serve and enjoy!

Nutrition:
Calories: 164 Carbs: 4.1g Sodium: 39.5mg
Fat: 1g Protein: 4g Potassium: 127.9mg

103. Delicious Aloo Palak

Preparation time: 10 minutes Cooking time: 6-8 hours Servings: 6

Ingredients:
- 2 pounds red potatoes, chopped
- 1 small onion, diced
- 1 red bell pepper, seeded and diced
- 1/4 cup fresh cilantro, chopped
- 1/3 cup low-sodium veggie broth
- 1/4 teaspoon salt
- 1/2 teaspoon Garam masala
- 1/2 teaspoon ground cumin
- 1/4 teaspoon ground turmeric
- 1/4 teaspoon ground coriander
- 1/4 teaspoon freshly ground black pepper
- 2 pounds fresh spinach, chopped

Directions:
1. Add potatoes, bell pepper, onion, cilantro, broth and seasoning to your Slow Cooker.
2. Mix well.
3. Add spinach on top.
4. Place the lid and cook on LOW for 6-8 hours.
5. Stir and serve.
6. Enjoy!

Nutrition:
Calories: 205 Carbs: 4g Sodium: 16.2mg
Fat: 1g; Protein: 9g Potassium: 197.4mg

104. Hasselback Eggplant Parmesan

Preparation time: 1 hour 10 minutes
Cooking time: 25 minutes
Servings: 2

Ingredients:
- 1 cup prepared low-sodium marinara sauce
- 4 small eggplants (about 6 inches long; 1 3/4 lbs. total)
- 2 tbsp. extra-virgin olive oil plus 2 tsp., divided
- 4 oz. fresh mozzarella, thinly sliced into 12 pieces
- 1/4 cup prepared pesto
- 1/2 cup whole-wheat panko breadcrumbs
- 2 tbsp. grated parmesan cheese
- 1 tbsp. chopped fresh basil

Directions:
1. Preheat the oven to 375F.
2. Spread the marinara sauce in a 9 x 13-inch baking dish.
3. Set crosswise cuts every 1/4 inch along each eggplant, slicing almost to the bottom but not all the way through.
4. Gently transfer the eggplants to the baking dish. Gently fan them to open the cuts wider. Drizzle 2 tbsp. of oil over the eggplants. Set the cuts alternately with mozzarella and pesto. Cover with foil.
5. Bake until the eggplants are very crispy, 45 to 55 minutes.
6. Merge the panko, parmesan, and the remaining oil in a small bowl. Detach the foil and sprinkle the eggplants with the breadcrumb mixture.
7. Change the oven setting to broil. Simmer the eggplants on the center rack until the topping is golden brown, 2 to 4 minutes. Set with the basil.

Nutrition:
Calories: 149 Carbs: 3g Sodium: 74 mg
Fat: 6g Protein: 8g Potassium: 150.5mg

105. Chicken Caesar Pasta Salad

Preparation time: 30 minutes
Cooking time: 20 minutes
Servings: 6

Ingredients:
- 1/2 cup low-fat buttermilk
- 1/4 cup low-fat plain Greek yogurt
- 3 tbsp. extra-virgin olive oil
- 2 tbsp. fresh lemon juice
- 2 tsp. Dijon mustard
- 1 1/2 tsp. anchovy paste
- 1 large garlic clove
- 3/4 cup grated parmesan cheese, divided
- 1/4 tsp. salt, divided
- 1/2 tsp. ground pepper, divided
- 8 oz. whole-wheat penne
- 3 cups shredded cooked chicken breast
- 1 pint cherry tomatoes, halved
- 5 cups chopped romaine lettuce

Directions:
1. Combine the buttermilk, yogurt, oil, lemon juice, mustard, anchovy paste, garlic, 1/2 cup parmesan, and 1/4 tsp. each of pepper and salt in a blender. Puree on high speed until smooth, about 1 minute. Set aside.
2. Process the pasta according to package directions, omitting salt. Drain, reserving 1 cup of the cooking water.
3. Combine the pasta, chicken, tomatoes, 1/4 cup of the reserved cooking water, and the remaining 1/4 tsp. each of pepper and salt.

4. Stir in the buttermilk dressing until thoroughly combined. Stir in the additional cooking water as needed for a creamy consistency.
5. Secure and chill for at least 30 minutes or up to 2 days.

Nutrition:

Calories: 209

Fat: 6g

Carbohydrates: 2.2g

Protein: 17g

Sodium: 94.7mg

Potassium: 191.6mg

Chapter 6. Snack

106. Pumpkin Pie Fat Bombs

Preparation Time: 35 minutes Cooking Time: 5 minutes Servings: 12

Ingredients:
- 2 tablespoons coconut oil
- 1/3 cup pumpkin puree
- 1/3 cup almond oil
- 1/4 cup almond oil
- 3 ounces sugar-free dark chocolate
- 1 1/2 teaspoon of pumpkin pie spice mix
- Stevia to taste

Directions:
1. Melt almond oil and dark chocolate over a double boiler. Take this mixture and layer the bottom of 12 muffin cups. Freeze until the crust has set. Meanwhile, take a saucepan and combine the rest of the ingredients.
2. Put the saucepan on low heat. Heat until softened and mix well. Pour this over the initial chocolate mixture. Let it chill for 1 hour, then serve.

Nutrition:
Calories: 124 Protein: 3g Sodium: 0mg
Carbs: 3g Fat: 13g Potassium: 142mg

107. Sweet Almond and Coconut Fat Bombs

Preparation Time: 10 minutes Cooking Time: 0 minutes Servings: 6

Ingredients:
- 1/4 cup melted coconut oil
- 9 1/2 tablespoons almond butter
- 90 drops liquid Stevia
- 3 tablespoons cocoa
- 9 tablespoons melted butter, salted

Directions:
1. Take a bowl and add all of the listed ingredients. Mix them well. Pour scant 2 tablespoons of the mixture into as many muffin molds as you like.
2. Chill for 20 minutes and pop them out. Serve and enjoy!

Nutrition:
Calories: 72 Protein: 2.53g Sodium: 0mg
Carbohydrates: 2g Fat: 14g Potassium: 188mg

108. Apricot Biscotti

Preparation Time: 10 minutes Cooking Time: 50 minutes Servings: 4

Ingredients:
- 2 tablespoons honey, dark
- 2 tablespoons olive oil
- 1/2 teaspoon almond extract
- 1/4 cup almonds, chopped roughly
- 2/3 cup apricots, dried
- 2 tablespoons milk, 1% and low-fat
- 2 eggs, beaten lightly
- 3/4 cup whole wheat flour
- 3/4 cup all-purpose flour
- 1/4 cup brown sugar, packed firm
- 1 teaspoon baking powder

Directions:
1. Warmth the oven to 350°F, then mix your baking powder, brown sugar, and flour in a bowl. Whisk your canola oil, eggs, almond extract, honey, and milk. Mix until it forms a smooth dough. Fold in the apricots and almonds.
2. Put your dough on plastic wrap, and then roll it out to a twelve-inch-long and three-inch wide rectangle. Set this dough on a baking sheet and bake for twenty-five minutes. It should turn golden

brown. Allow it to cool, slice it into 1/2 inch thick slices, and then bake for another fifteen minutes. It should be crispy.

Nutrition:
Calories: 291   Sodium: 123mg   Protein: 2g
Fat: 2g   Carbs: 12g   Potassium: 159mg

109. Apple and Berry Cobbler

Preparation Time: 10 minutes   Cooking Time: 40 minutes   Servings: 4

Ingredients:

Filling:
- 1 cup blueberries, fresh
- 2 cups apples, chopped
- 1 cup raspberries, fresh
- 2 tablespoons brown sugar
- 1 teaspoon lemon zest
- 2 teaspoon lemon juice, fresh
- 1/2 teaspoon ground cinnamon
- 1 1/2 tablespoons cornstarch

Topping:
- 3/4 cup whole wheat pastry flour
- 1 1/2 tablespoon brown sugar
- 1/2 teaspoon vanilla extract
- 1/4 cup soy milk
- 1/4 teaspoon sea salt, fine
- 1 egg white

Directions:
1. Set on your oven to 350 and get out six small ramekins. Grease them with cooking spray. Mix your lemon juice, lemon zest, blueberries, sugar, cinnamon, raspberries, and apples in a bowl. Stir in your cornstarch, mixing until it dissolves.
2. Beat your egg white in a different bowl, whisking it with sugar, vanilla, soy milk, and pastry flour. Divide your berry mixture between the ramekins and top with the vanilla topping. Put your ramekins on a baking sheet, baking for thirty minutes. The top should be golden brown before serving.

Nutrition:
Calories: 131   Sodium: 14mg   Protein: 7.2g
Fat: 0g   Carbs: 3.8g   Potassium: 155mg

110. Mixed Fruit Compote Cups

Preparation Time: 5 minutes   Cooking Time: 15 minutes   Servings: 2

Ingredients:
- 1 1/4 cup water
- 1/2 cup orange juice
- 12 ounces mixed dried fruit
- 1 teaspoon ground cinnamon
- 1/4 teaspoon ground ginger
- 1/4 teaspoon ground nutmeg
- 4 cups vanilla frozen yogurt, fat-free

Directions:
1. Mix your dried fruit, nutmeg, cinnamon, water, orange juice, and ginger in a saucepan.
2. Cover, and allow it to cook over medium heat for ten minutes. Remove the cover and then cook for another ten minutes.
3. Add your frozen yogurt to serving cups, and top with the fruit mixture.

Nutrition:
Calories: 228   Sodium: 114mg   Protein: 9.1g
Fat: 5.7g   Carbs: 2.4g   Potassium: 143.8mg

111. Generous Garlic Bread Stick

Preparation time: 15 minutes Cooking time: 15 minutes Servings: 8

Ingredients:
- 1/4 cup almond butter, softened
- 1 teaspoon garlic powder
- 2 cups almond flour
- 1/2 tablespoon baking powder
- 1 tablespoon psyllium husk powder
- 1/4 teaspoon sunflower seeds
- 3 tablespoons almond butter, melted
- 1 egg
- 1/4 cup boiling water

Directions:
1. Preheat your oven to 400F.
2. Line the baking sheet with parchment paper and keep it on the side.
3. Beat almond butter with garlic powder and keep it on the side.
4. Add almond flour, baking powder, husk, sunflower seeds in a bowl and mix in almond butter and egg, mix well.
5. Pour boiling water in the mix and stir until you have a nice dough.
6. Divide the dough into 8 balls and roll into breadsticks.
7. Set on a baking sheet and process for 15 minutes.
8. Brush each stick with garlic almond butter and bake for 5 minutes more.
9. Serve and enjoy!

Nutrition:
Calories: 159 Protein: 7g Sodium: 24mg
Carbs: 7g Fat: 24g Potassium: 182mg

112. Cauliflower Bread Stick

Preparation time: 10 minutes Cooking time: 48 minutes Servings: 5

Ingredients:
- 1 cup cashew cheese/kite ricotta cheese
- 1 tablespoon organic almond butter
- 1 whole egg
- 1/2 teaspoon Italian seasoning
- 1/4 teaspoon red pepper flakes
- 1/8 teaspoon kosher sunflower seeds
- 2 cups cauliflower rice, cooked for 3 minutes in microwave
- 3 teaspoons garlic, minced
- Parmesan cheese, grated

Directions:
1. Preheat your oven to 350F.
2. Add almond butter in a small pan and melt over low heat
3. Add red pepper flakes, garlic to the almond butter and cook for 2-3 minutes.
4. Add garlic and almond butter mix to the bowl with cooked cauliflower and add the Italian seasoning.
5. Season with sunflower seeds and mix, refrigerate for 10 minutes.
6. Add cheese and eggs to the bowl and mix.
7. Place a layer of parchment paper at the bottom of a 9x9 baking dish and grease with cooking spray, add egg and mozzarella cheese mix to the cauliflower mix.
8. Add mix to the pan and smooth to a thin layer with the palms of your hand.
9. Bake for 30 minutes, take out from the oven and top with a few shakes of parmesan and mozzarella.
10. Cook for 8 minutes more.
11. Enjoy!

Nutrition:
Calories: 149 Protein: 10.7g Sodium: 5mg
Carbs: 11.5g Fat: 20g Potassium: 192.6mg

Dash Diet Cookbook

113. Cocktail Wieners

Preparation time: 2 minutes Cooking Time: 1 minutes Servings: 12

Ingredients:
- 1 package 12 cocktail wieners
- 1/4 teaspoon brown sugar
- 1/2 cup chicken or veggie broth
- 1 jar jalapeño jelly
- 1/4 cup chili sauce
- 1 diced jalapeño

Directions:
1. Put 1/2 cup of chicken broth into an instant pot, then add wieners and rest of ingredients, still till everything is coated.
2. Cook on high pressure for a minute, quick release pressure then serve!

Nutrition:
Calories: 92
Fat: 5g
Carbs: 6g
Protein: 10g
Sodium: 4mg
Potassium: 176.3mg

114. Pressure Cooker Braised Pulled Ham

Preparation time: 10 minutes Cooking Time: 25 minutes Servings: 16

Ingredients:
- 2 bottles beer, or nonalcoholic beer
- 1/2 teaspoon coarse ground pepper
- 1 cup Dijon mustard, divided
- 1 cooked bone-in ham
- 16 split pretzel hamburger buns
- 4 rosemary sprigs
- dill pickle slices

Directions:
1. Whisk the beer, pepper and mustard, and then add ham and rosemary, lock the lid, and process pressure to high for 20 minutes, then natural pressure release.
2. Let it cool, discard rosemary, and skim the fat, and then let it boil for 5 minutes.
3. When ham is cool, shred with forks, discard bone, heat it again, and then put the ham on the pretzel buns, adding Dijon mustard at the end and the dill pickle slices.

Nutrition:
Calories: 378
Fat: 9g
Carbs: 5g
Protein: 25g
Sodium: 7mg
Potassium: 179mg

115. Mini Teriyaki Turkey Sandwiches

Preparation time: 20 minutes Cooking Time: 30 minutes Servings: 20

Ingredients:
- 2 chicken breast halves
- 1 cup soy sauce, low-salt
- 1/4 cup cider vinegar
- 3 minced garlic cloves
- 1 tablespoon fresh ginger root
- 2 tablespoons cornstarch
- 20 Hawaiian sweet rolls
- 1/2 teaspoon pepper
- 2 tablespoons melted butter

Directions:
1. Put the turkey in a pressure cooker and combine the first six ingredients over it.
2. Cook it on manual for 25 minutes, and when finished, natural pressure release.
3. Push sauté after removing the turkey, then mix cornstarch and water, stirring into cooking juices, and cook until sauce is thickened. Shred meat and stir to heat.
4. You can split the rolls, buttering each side, and bake till golden brown, adding the meat mixture to the top.

Nutrition:
Calories: 252 Carbs: 5g Sodium: 42mg
Fat: 5g Protein: 26g Potassium: 186.3mg

116. Peach Crumble Muffins

Preparation Time: 25 minutes Cooking Time: 25 minutes Servings: 12

Ingredients:
For the crumble:
- 2 tablespoons dark brown sugar
- 1 tablespoon honey
- 1 teaspoon ground cinnamon
- 2 tablespoons canola oil
- 1/2 cup old-fashioned rolled oats

For the peach muffins:
- 1 teaspoon baking powder
- 1 teaspoon baking soda
- 1 teaspoon ground cinnamon
- 1/2 teaspoon ground ginger
- 1/4 teaspoon kosher or sea salt
- 1/4 cup canola oil
- 1/4 cup dark brown sugar
- 2 large eggs
- 1 1/2 teaspoons vanilla extract
- 1/4 cup plain nonfat Greek yogurt
- 3 peaches, diced (about 1 1/2 cups)
- 1 3/4 cups whole wheat flour or whole wheat pastry flour

Directions:
1. In a small bowl, mix the brown sugar, honey, cinnamon, canola oil, and oats until combined for the crumble. For your muffins, mix the flour, baking powder, baking soda, cinnamon, ginger, and salt in a large bowl.
2. Beat the canola oil, brown sugar, and one egg at a time in a separate bowl, using a hand mixer until fluffy. Beat in the vanilla extract and yogurt. Put the flour mixture in the bowl and whisk until the ingredients are just combined.
3. Fold in the diced peaches with a spatula. Preheat the oven to 425°F. Oil a 12-cup muffin tin with muffin liners. Fill each muffin cup with batter about three-quarters of the way full. Scoop the crumble batter on top of each.
4. Bake for 5 to 6 minutes, then reduce the oven temperature to 350°F and bake for 15 to 18 additional minutes. Cool before removing from the muffin tin. Once completely cooled, serve.

Nutrition:
Calories: 187 Carbs: 6g Sodium: 26mg
Fat: 8g Protein: 4g Potassium: 182.7mg

117. Cranberry Hot Wings

Preparation time: 45 minutes Cooking Time: 35 minutes Servings: 4 dozen

Ingredients:
- 1 can jellied cranberry sauce
- 1/4 cup Louisiana-style hot sauce
- 2 tablespoons honey
- 1 tablespoon Dijon mustard
- 1/2 cup sugar-free orange juice
- 2 tablespoons soy sauce
- 2 teaspoons garlic powder
- 1 minced garlic clove
- 1 teaspoon dried minced onion
- 5 pounds chicken wings
- 1/4 teaspoon salt
- 2 tablespoons cold water
- 4 teaspoons cornstarch

Directions:
1. Whisk the ingredients together but discard wing tips.
2. Put the wins in your instant pot, and then put cranberry mixture over top.
3. Lock the lid, and then adjust pressure to high for 10 minutes.

4. You can from there, natural pressure release, and quick pressure.
5. Preheat broiler, skim fat, and from there, let it broil for 20-25 minutes.
6. When browned, brush with the glaze before serving

Nutrition:

Calories: 71 Carbs: 5g Sodium: 35mg
Fat: 4g Protein: 5g Potassium: 148.2mg

118. Almond and Tomato Balls

Preparation Time: 10 minutes Cooking Time: 0 minutes Servings: 6

Ingredients:
- 1/3 cup pistachios, de-shelled
- 1/3 cup sun-dried tomatoes, diced
- 10 ounces cream cheese

Directions:
1. Chop pistachios into small pieces. Add cream cheese, tomatoes in a bowl and mix well. Chill for 15-20 minutes and turn into balls. Roll into pistachios. Serve and enjoy!

Nutrition:

Calories: 183 Carbs: 5g Sodium: 10mg
Fat: 18g Protein: 5g Potassium: 184.7mg

119. Avocado Tuna Bites

Preparation Time: 10 minutes Cooking Time: 0 minutes Servings: 4

Ingredients:
- 1/3 cup coconut oil
- 1 avocado, cut into cubes
- 10 ounces of canned tuna, drained
- 1/4 cup Parmesan cheese, grated
- 1/4 teaspoon garlic powder
- 1/4 teaspoon onion powder
- 1/3 cup almond flour
- 1/4 teaspoon pepper
- 1/4 cup low-fat mayonnaise
- Pepper as needed

Directions:
1. Take a bowl and add tuna, mayo, flour, parmesan, spices, and mix well. Fold in avocado and make 12 balls out of the mixture.
2. Dissolve coconut oil in a pan and cook over medium heat until all sides are golden. Serve and enjoy!

Nutrition:

Calories: 185 Carbs: 1g Sodium: 0mg
Fat: 18g Protein: 5g Potassium: 128.3mg

120. Hearty Buttery Walnuts

Preparation Time: 10 minutes Cooking Time: 0 minutes Servings: 4

Ingredients:
- 4 walnut halves
- 1/2 tablespoon almond butter

Directions:
1. Spread butter over two walnut halves.
2. Top with other halves. Serve and enjoy!

Nutrition:

Calories: 90 Carbs: 0g Sodium: 1 mg
Fat: 10g Protein: 1g Potassium: 129.4mg

121. Refreshing Watermelon Sorbet

Preparation Time: 20 minutes + 20 hours chill time
Cooking Time: 0 minutes
Servings: 4

Ingredients:
- 4 cups watermelon, seedless and chunked
- 1/4 cup of coconut sugar
- 2 tablespoons lime juice

Directions:
1. Add the listed fixing to a blender and puree. Freeze the mix for about 4-6 hours until you have gelatin-like consistency.
2. Puree the mix once again in batches and return to the container. Chill overnight. Allow the sorbet to stand for 5 minutes before serving and enjoy!

Nutrition:
Calories: 91
Fat: 0g
Carbs: 5g
Protein: 1g
Sodium: 0mg
Potassium: 138.2mg

122. Faux Mac and Cheese

Preparation Time: 15 minutes
Cooking Time: 45 minutes
Servings: 4

Ingredients:
- 5 cups cauliflower florets
- 1/4tsp. salt and pepper to taste
- 1 cup of coconut milk
- 1/2 cup vegetable broth
- 2 tablespoons coconut flour, sifted
- 1 organic egg, beaten
- 2 cups cheddar cheese

Directions:
1. Warm your oven to 350F. Season florets with salt and steam until firm. Place florets in a greased ovenproof dish. Heat-up coconut milk over medium heat in a skillet; make sure to season the oil with salt and pepper.
2. Stir in broth and add coconut flour to the mix, stir. Cook until the sauce begins to bubble. Remove heat and add beaten egg. Pour the thick sauce over cauliflower and mix in cheese. Bake for 30-45 minutes. Serve and enjoy!

Nutrition:
Calories: 229
Fat: 14g
Carbs: 9g
Protein: 15g
Sodium: 25mg
Potassium: 158.2mg

123. Banana Custard

Preparation Time: 10 minutes
Cooking Time: 25 minutes
Servings: 3

Ingredients:
- 2 ripe bananas, peeled and mashed finely
- 1/2 teaspoon of vanilla extract
- 14 ounces unsweetened almond milk
- 3 eggs

Directions:
1. Warm your oven to 350F. Grease 8 custard glasses lightly. Arrange the glasses in a large baking dish. Take a large bowl and mix all of the ingredients and mix them well until combined nicely.
2. Divide the mixture evenly between the glasses. Pour water into the baking dish. Bake for 25 minutes. Take out and serve.

Nutrition:
Calories: 59
Fat: 2.4g
Carbs: 7g
Protein: 3g
Sodium: 92mg
Potassium: 127.1mg

124. Healthy Tahini Buns

Preparation Time: 10 minutes Cooking Time: 15-20 minutes Servings: 3

Ingredients:
- 1 whole egg
- 5 tablespoons tahini paste
- 1/2 teaspoon baking soda
- 1 teaspoon lemon juice
- 1/4tsp. of salt

Directions:
1. Warm your oven to 350F. Set a baking sheet with parchment paper and keep it on the side. Put the listed fixing in a blender and blend until you have a smooth batter.
2. Scoop batter into prepared sheet forming buns. Bake for 15-20 minutes. Remove, then let them cool. Serve and enjoy!

Nutrition:
Calories: 172 Protein: 6g Sodium: 12mg
Carbs: 7g Fat: 14g Potassium: 132mg

125. Sautéed Swiss Chard

Preparation time: 5 minutes Cooking time: 10 minutes Servings: 6

Ingredients:
- 15 oz swiss chard, chopped
- 1/2 cup of soy milk
- 1 teaspoon chili powder
- 1 tablespoon avocado oil
- 1 teaspoon whole-grain wheat flour
- 1/4 onion, diced

Directions:
1. Warm the avocado oil in a pan and add the onion. Sauté for 3 minutes.
2. Stir well and add flour and soy milk. Whisk the mixture until smooth.
3. Add the chard and gently remix the ingredients.
4. Close the lid and sauté the side dish for 5 minutes over medium-low heat.

Nutrition:
Calories: 40 Carbs: 5 g Sodium: 150 mg
Fat: 1 g Protein: 3 g Potassium: 220 mg

126. Asian Style Asparagus

Preparation time: 5 minutes Cooking time: 10 minutes Servings: 2

Ingredients:
- 8 oz. asparagus, chopped
- 1 tablespoon balsamic vinegar
- 1 teaspoon lime zest, grated
- 1 teaspoon sesame seeds
- 1/4 teaspoon ground cumin
- 2 tablespoons olive oil

Directions:
1. Put 1 tbsp. of olive oil in a skillet and attach the chopped asparagus.
2. Add the lime zest and roast the vegetables for 5 minutes. Stir once in a while.
3. Next, sprinkle the vegetables with ground cumin and add the remaining oil.
4. Bake the asparagus for 5 minutes at 400F in the oven.
5. Then, drizzle the cooked vegetables with balsamic vinegar and sesame seeds. Shake the side dish well.

Nutrition:
Calories: 130 Carbs: 5 g Sodium: 30 mg
Fat: 1 g Protein: 3 g Potassium: 150 mg

127. Aromatic Cauliflower Florets

Preparation time: 7 minutes Cooking time: 18 minutes Servings: 6

Ingredients:
- 1-pound cauliflower florets
- 1 tablespoon curry powder
- 1/4 cup of soy milk
- 1 tablespoon oil
- 1/2 teaspoon dried oregano

Directions:
1. Preheat the oven to 375F.
2. Heat the oil in a saucepan.
3. Combine soy milk and curry powder and whisk the liquid until smooth.
4. Pour it into the saucepan with the oil and bring to a boil.
5. Add cauliflower florets and stir well.
6. Then, close the lid and cook the vegetables for 5 minutes. Transfer the pan to the preheated oven and cook the meal for 10 minutes, until the florets are soft.

Nutrition:
Calories 80 Carbs 10 g Sodium 60 mg
Fat 2 g Protein 2 g Potassium 270 mg

128. Brussel Sprouts Mix

Preparation time: 6 minutes Cooking time: 15 minutes Servings: 2

Ingredients:
- 1 cup Brussel sprouts, sliced
- 1 tablespoon olive oil
- 1 tomato, chopped
- 1/2 cup fresh parsley, chopped
- 2 oz. leek, sliced
- 1 cup vegetable broth
- 1/2 jalapeno pepper, chopped

Directions:
1. Pour the olive oil into a saucepan.
2. Add the sliced Brussels sprouts and leek and cook for 5 minutes. Stir the vegetables occasionally.
3. Add the parsley, chopped tomato, jalapeno, and vegetable broth.
4. Close the lid and cook at medium-high heat for 10 min. Stir the vegetables during cooking to avoid burning them.

Nutrition:
Calories: 65 Carbs: 15 g Sodium: 160 mg
Fat: 4 g Protein: 3 g Potassium: 140 mg

129. Braised Baby Carrot

Preparation time: 5 minutes Cooking time: 22 minutes Servings: 2

Ingredients:
- 1 cup baby carrots
- 1 teaspoon dried thyme
- 1 tablespoon olive oil
- 1/2 cup vegetable stock
- 1 garlic clove, sliced

Directions:
1. Heat the olive oil in the saucepan for 30 seconds.
2. Then add the sliced garlic and dried thyme. Set the mixture to a boil and add the baby carrot.
3. Roast the vegetables for 7 min over medium heat. Stir them constantly.
4. Then, add vegetable stock and close the lid.
5. Cook the baby carrots for 15 min until they are tender.

Nutrition:
Calories: 69 Carbs: 1 g Sodium: 10 mg
Fat: 5 g Protein: 2 g Potassium: 140 mg

130. Acorn Squash with Apples

Preparation time: 20-25 minutes Cooking time: 5-7 minutes
Servings: 2

Ingredients:
- 1 Granny Smith apple
- 2 tablespoons brown sugar
- 1 Acorn squash, small or about 6 inches in diameter
- 2 teaspoons margarine - trans-fat-free

Directions:
1. Peel the apple, then remove the core and slice.
2. Toss the apple and brown sugar. Set aside.
3. Poke a few holes in the squash. Place it into the microwave for 5 min using the high-power setting.
4. Turn the squash over after three minutes.
5. Put it on the chopping block and slice it in half. Discard the seeds and load the hollowed squash with the apple mixture.
6. Set the container back in the microwave and continue cooking the apples until they're softened (2 min.).
7. Serve the squash with a portion of margarine.

Nutrition:
Calories: 209 Carbs: 3.2 g Sodium: 25 mg
Fat: 4 g Protein: 3 g Potassium: 50 mg

131. Asparagus with Horseradish Dip

Preparation time: 15 minutes Cooking time: 5 minutes Servings: 16

Ingredients:
- 32 (about 2 lb.) fresh asparagus spears
- 1 cup reduced-fat mayonnaise
- 1/4 cup parmesan cheese - grated
- 1 tablespoon prepared horseradish
- 1/2 teaspoon Worcestershire sauce

Directions:
1. Trim and place the asparagus in a steamer basket in a large saucepan (over one inch of water).
2. Wait for it to boil by covering. Steam until crisp-tender (2-4 min.).
3. Drain and immediately place it into ice water to chill. Drain it into a colander and pat dry.
4. Combine the rest of the dressings.
5. Serve with the asparagus.

Nutrition:
Calories: 129 Carbs: 2 g Sodium: 10 mg
Fat: 8 g Protein: 5 g Potassium: 107 mg

132. Grilled Tomatoes

Preparation time: 10 minutes Cooking time: 2 minutes Servings: 4

Ingredients:
- 4 tomatoes
- 1/2 teaspoon dried basil
- 1 tablespoon olive oil
- 1/2 teaspoon dried oregano

Directions:
1. Preheat the grill to 390F.
2. Slice the tomatoes and sprinkle with dried oregano and dried basil.
3. Then, drizzle the vegetables with olive oil and place them in the preheated grill.

4. Grill the tomatoes for 1 minute on each side.
5. Use a metal scoop to lift the tomatoes off the grill. Serve.

Nutrition:

Calories: 115 | Carbs: 5 g | Sodium: 30 mg
Fat: 4 g | Protein: 6 g | Potassium: 107 mg

133. Parsley Celery Root

Preparation time: 7 minutes | Cooking time: 20 minutes | Servings: 4

Ingredients:
- 2 cups celery root, chopped
- 2 oz. fresh parsley, chopped
- 1 tablespoon margarine
- 1 teaspoon olive oil
- 1 teaspoon cumin seeds
- 1/4 cup of water

Directions:
1. Mix up olive oil and margarine in the skillet.
2. Add cumin seeds and heat the mixture for 1-2 minutes or until you get the light cumin smell.
3. Then, add chopped celery root and roast it for 8 minutes (for 4 minutes from each side).
4. Then add water and parsley. Close the lid.
5. Cook the vegetables for 8 minutes on medium-low heat or until it is tender.

Nutrition:

Calories: 132 | Carbs: 1.6 g | Sodium: 10 mg
Fat: 2 g | Protein: 3 g | Potassium: 127 mg

134. Garlic Black Eyed Peas

Preparation Time: 10 minutes | Cooking Time: 120 minutes | Servings: 4

Ingredients:
- 2 garlic cloves, diced
- 1/3 cup black eye peas, soaked
- 1 tablespoon shallot, chopped
- 1 tablespoon avocado oil
- 1 teaspoon cayenne pepper
- 2 cups water

Directions:
1. In a skillet, mix garlic, shallot, cayenne pepper and avocado oil.
2. Sautè the mixture for 1 minute.
3. Add black eye peas and water.
4. Then, close the lid and cook the meal over low heat for 2 hours or until the black eye is soft.

Nutrition:

Calories: 135 | Carbs: 2.6 g | Sodium: 16 mg
Fat: 2 g | Protein: 5 g | Potassium: 157 mg

135. Braised Artichokes

Preparation time: 15 minutes | Cooking time: 35 minutes | Servings: 4

Ingredients:
- 4 artichokes, trimmed
- 4 garlic cloves, minced
- 4 tablespoons olive oil
- 1 lemon
- 1 cup of water
- 1 teaspoon dried cilantro
- 1/2 teaspoon dried basil

Directions:
1. Squash the juice from the lemon into the saucepan.
2. Add water.
3. Then, in the shallow bowl, mix up garlic, olive oil, dried cilantro, and dried basil.
4. Rub the artichokes with the garlic mixture and place them in the lemon and water.

5. Close lid and cook vegetables for 35 minutes or until tender.
6. Drizzle the cooked artichokes with the lemon and water mixture. Serve.

Nutrition:

Calories: 205 Carbs: 19 g Sodium: 26 mg
Fat: 12 g Protein: 3 g Potassium: 131 mg

136. Grilled Eggplant Slices

Preparation time: 10 minutes Cooking time: 15-20 minutes Servings: 4

Ingredients:
- 2 eggplants
- 1 fresh chili pepper
- 1 garlic clove
- 1/4 teaspoon dried dill
- 5 tablespoons extra virgin olive oil
- 1/4tsp. salt
- black pepper

Directions:
1. Wash the eggplants and dry them well. Divide them into slices about half an inch thick.
2. Heat a grill pan and place the eggplant slices in it, a few at a time.
3. Let them grill for a few minutes, first on one side and then on the other. Set them on a plate as they are ready.
4. Prepare the marinade: pour the oil into a small bowl, add a pinch of salt and ground pepper, the chopped garlic clove and a pinch of finely chopped chili pepper. Stir everything with a fork until the salt is completely dissolved.
5. Brush the eggplants with the marinade and arrange them in layers on a serving plate. Let the grilled eggplant rest before serving.

Nutrition:

Calories: 85 Carbs: 4 g Sodium: 26 mg
Fat: 1 g Protein: 3 g Potassium: 47 mg

137. Lentil Sauté

Preparation time: 5 minutes Cooking time: 40 minutes Servings: 4

Ingredients:
- 1/2 cup lentils
- 1 cup spinach
- 4 cups of water
- 1 teaspoon cayenne pepper
- 1/2 teaspoon ground coriander
- 1 garlic clove
- 1 tomato, chopped

Directions:
1. Mix all ingredients in a saucepan and stir them gently.
2. Cover and cook the sauté for 40 minutes on medium-high heat.

Nutrition:

Calories 115 Carbs 17 g Sodium 16 mg
Fat 2 g Protein 7 g Potassium 128 mg

138. Italian Style Zucchini Coins

Preparation time: 10 minutes Cooking time: 5 minutes Servings: 2

Ingredients:
- 2 zucchinis, sliced
- 1 tablespoon Italian seasonings
- 2 tablespoons olive oil
- 1/4 teaspoon garlic powder

Directions:
1. Dip the zucchini slices with Italian seasonings and garlic powder.
2. Then warmth the olive oil in a skillet.

3. Place the zucchini rings in the pan in a single layer and cook for 1 min from each side or until lightly browned.
4. Set the zucchini with the help of a paper towel.

Nutrition:

Calories 105   Carbs: 3.7 g   Sodium: 6 mg

Fat: 0.5 g   Protein: 1 g   Potassium: 114 mg

139. Brussels sprouts with Shallots and Lemon

Preparation time: 25 minutes   Cooking time: 10 minutes   Servings: 4

Ingredients:
- 3 teaspoon Olive oil - divided
- 3 tbsp. Shallots, sliced thin
- 1/4 teaspoon Salt - divided
- 1 lb. Brussels sprouts
- 1/2 Vegetable stock/broth - no-salt
- 1/4 Lemon zest - finely grated
- 1 tablespoon Lemon juice - fresh squeezed
- 1/4 teaspoon Black pepper

Directions:
1. Warm a large, nonstick skillet to heat two teaspoons of oil using the medium temperature setting. Add and sauté the shallots until softened and lightly golden (6 min.)
2. Stir in salt (1/4tsp.). Transfer to a bowl and set aside.
3. In the same pan, warm the rest of the oil (1 tsp.) over medium heat.
4. Cut the Brussels sprouts into quarters. Add them to the pan to sauté them for three to four minutes.
5. Add the vegetable stock and wait for it to heat. Simmer with the top of the pan until the Brussels sprouts are tender or about five to six minutes.
6. Scoop the shallots into the pan, mix in the lemon zest and juice, pepper, and the rest of the salt (1/4 tsp.).
7. Enjoy them right away.

Nutrition:

Calories: 155   Carbs: 1.9 g   Sodium: 17 mg

Fat: 3.5 g   Protein: 8 g   Potassium: 134 mg

140. Chili-Lime Grilled Pineapple

Preparation Time: 15 minutes   Cooking time: 2-6 minutes   Servings: 6

Ingredients:
- 1 Fresh pineapple
- 1 tablespoon Honey/agave nectar
- 3 tablespoon Brown sugar
- 1 tablespoon Lime juice
- 1 tablespoon Olive oil
- 1/4 teaspoon Salt
- 1 1/2 Chili powder

Directions:
1. Peel pineapple, removing any eyes from fruit. Cut lengthwise into six wedges; remove the core.
2. Blend remaining ingredients until combined. Garnish the pineapple with half of the glaze; reserve remaining mixture for basting.
3. Grill the pineapple using the medium temperature setting and cover. You may also choose to bake it until lightly browned (2-4 min. per side), basting occasionally with the reserved glaze.

Nutrition:

Calories: 105   Carbs: 1.9 g   Sodium: 37 mg

Fat: 2 g   Protein: 8 g   Potassium: 134 mg

Chapter 7. Veggies

141. Zucchini Fritters with Corn Salsa

Preparation Time: 10 minutes Cooking time: 10 minutes Servings: 4

Ingredients:

For the salsa:
- 2 cups cherry tomatoes, diced, juices reserved
- 1 shallot, diced
- 1 cup corn kernels (thawed, if frozen)
- 1/2 cup chopped fresh cilantro
- 1 tablespoon freshly squeezed lime juice
- 1 tablespoon extra-virgin olive oil
- Freshly ground black pepper

For the fritters
- 2 large zucchini, grated, about 4 cups
- 1 or 15-ounce can low-sodium cannellini beans, rinsed and drained
- 2 large egg whites
- 3 tablespoons chopped fresh parsley
- 2 garlic cloves, minced
- 1/4 teaspoon sea salt
- 1/2 cup almond flour

Directions:

To make the salsa
1. In a medium bowl, set together the tomatoes, shallot, corn, cilantro, lime juice, and olive oil. Season with pepper to taste. Set aside for 30 minutes so flavors will meld.

To make the fritters
1. Preheat the air fryer to 370F.
2. Using a dish towel or paper towel, pat the grated zucchini dry to remove any excess water.
3. In a bowl, use a fork to merge the zucchini, beans, egg whites, parsley, garlic, salt, and almond flour. Slightly mash the beans while mixing. Using damp hands, form the zucchini mixture into 16 patties.
4. Working in batches if necessary, set the patties in a single layer in the air fryer basket and cook for 12 minutes, until golden brown. Serve the fritters topped with salsa.

Nutrition:

Calories: 228 Sodium: 114mg Protein: 9.1g
Fat: 5.7g Carbs: 2.4g Potassium: 143.8mg

142. Zucchini Lasagna Roll-Ups

Preparation Time: 20 minutes Cooking time: 10 minutes Servings: 4

Ingredients:
- 2 cups part-skim ricotta cheese
- 1/2 cup low-sodium cannellini beans, drained, rinsed, and mashed
- 2 cups fresh spinach
- 2 tablespoons granulated garlic, divided
- 2 tablespoons dried basil, divided
- 2 tablespoons dried oregano, divided
- 2 teaspoons freshly ground black pepper, divided
- 2 large zucchini, cut lengthwise into ⅛-inch-thick strips
- 2 cups unsweetened almond milk
- 1 tablespoon extra-virgin olive oil
- 1 cup whole wheat panko bread crumbs
- Extra-virgin olive oil cooking spray
- 2 cups low-sodium marinara sauce

Directions:
1. Preheat the air fryer to 400F.
2. In a medium bowl, set together the ricotta cheese, mashed beans, spinach, 1 tablespoon of garlic powder, 1 tablespoon of basil, 1 tablespoon of oregano, and 1 teaspoon of pepper.
3. Lay the zucchini slices flat in a single layer. Spread 1 tablespoon of the ricotta mixture along each zucchini slice. Roll up each slice and secure with a toothpick.

4. In a separate bowl, set together the almond milk and olive oil.
5. In a bowl, stir together the panko bread crumbs with the remaining 1 tablespoon of garlic powder, 1 tablespoon of basil, 1 tablespoon of oregano, and 1 teaspoon of pepper.
6. One at a time, dunk each zucchini roll-up into the almond milk mixture and then coat in the panko bread crumb mixture. Repeat until all are coated.
7. Working in batches if necessary, place each zucchini roll-up in the air fryer basket in a single layer, mist with the olive oil, and cook for 10 minutes.
8. While the zucchini roll-ups are cooking, heat the marinara sauce on the stovetop over medium heat until warm. Serve the zucchini roll-ups topped with marinara sauce.

Nutrition:
Calories: 205　　　Carbs: 4g　　　Sodium: 16.2mg
Fat: 1g;　　　Protein: 9g　　　Potassium: 197.4mg

143. Toasted Chickpea-Quinoa Bowl

Preparation Time: 20 minutes　　　Cooking time: 10 minutes　　　Servings: 4

Ingredients:
For the vinaigrette
- 2 tablespoons freshly squeezed lemon juice
- 2 tablespoons extra-virgin olive oil
- 1 tablespoon white wine vinegar
- 1 tablespoon Italian seasoning
- 1 teaspoon Dijon mustard
- 1 teaspoon freshly ground black pepper

For the chickpea-quinoa bowl
- 1 (15-ounce) can low-sodium chickpeas, drained and rinsed
- 2 large zucchini, chopped
- 3 cups coarsely chopped cauliflower florets
- 1 tablespoon extra-virgin olive oil
- 1 teaspoon paprika
- 1 teaspoon garlic powder
- 1 teaspoon ground cumin
- 1/2 cup dry quinoa
- 4 cups fresh arugula

Directions:
To make the vinaigrette
1. In a small bowl, set together the lemon juice, olive oil, and vinegar. Add the Italian seasoning, mustard, and black pepper and whisk again.

To make the chickpea-quinoa bowl
1. In a bowl, stir together the chickpeas, zucchini, cauliflower, olive oil, paprika, garlic powder, and cumin.
2. Working in batches if necessary, place the chickpea and vegetable mixture in the air fryer basket in a single layer. Set the temperature to 350F and process for 4 minutes. Shake or stir and cook for 4 minutes, until the vegetables are tender.
3. Process the quinoa according to the package directions.
4. To assemble, divide the quinoa and arugula between bowls, top with the chickpeas and vegetables, and drizzle with the vinaigrette.

Nutrition:
Calories: 214　　　Carbs: 2 g　　　Sodium: 15 mg
Fat: 8 g　　　Protein: 30 g　　　Potassium: 121 mg

144. Fried Pasta Chips with Tomato-Basil Dip

Preparation Time: 20 minutes　　　Cooking time: 15 minutes　　　Servings: 4

Ingredients:
For the tomato-basil dip
- 1 bunch fresh basil, stemmed
- 1 tablespoon extra-virgin olive oil

- 1 garlic clove
- 1/2 cup pine nuts
- 1 tablespoon freshly squeezed lemon juice
- 1/4 cup cherry tomatoes

For the pasta chips
- 12 ounces chickpea pasta
- 2 tablespoons extra-virgin olive oil
- 4 tablespoons nutritional yeast
- 1 teaspoon dried basil
- 1/4 teaspoon sea salt
- 1 to 2 teaspoons water (optional)
- Freshly ground black pepper
- 1 teaspoon dried oregano
- 1 teaspoon granulated garlic
- 1/4 teaspoon sea salt

Directions:

To make the tomato-basil dip
1. In a high-speed blender or food processor, merge the basil, olive oil, garlic, pine nuts, lemon juice, tomatoes, and salt and blend on high speed until well mixed. If the mixture appears dry, add the water. Season with pepper to taste.

To make the pasta chips
1. Preheat the air fryer to 375°F.
2. Set a pot of water to a boil. Cook the pasta at a boil, stirring occasionally, until al dente, about 8 minutes.
3. Bring the pasta to a large bowl and drizzle with the olive oil. Stir in the nutritional yeast, basil, oregano, garlic, and salt.
4. Working in batches if necessary, place the pasta in the air fryer basket in a single layer and cook for 5 minutes. Shake or stir when the timer goes off, then continue to cook for another 2 to 3 minutes, until the pasta is golden brown.
5. Transfer to a paper-towel–lined plate and allow to cool before serving alongside the tomato-basil dip.

Nutrition:
Calories: 499　　　　Fat: 20g　　　　Sodium: 30mg
Carbs: 57g　　　　Protein: 23g　　　　Potassium: 107 mg

145. Penne with Sizzling Tomatoes and Artichokes

Preparation Time: 20 minutes　　　Cooking time: 10 minutes　　　Servings: 4

Ingredients:
- 12 ounces chickpea penne
- 4 cups cherry tomatoes
- 1 (7-ounce) jar marinated artichoke hearts, drained and chopped
- 2 tablespoons extra-virgin olive oil
- 1 tablespoon dried basil
- 1 tablespoon dried oregano
- 2 teaspoons granulated garlic

Directions:
1. Preheat the air fryer to 375F. Process the pasta according to the package directions.
2. In a large bowl, stir together the tomatoes, artichoke hearts, olive oil, basil, oregano, and garlic.
3. Set the air fryer basket with parchment paper or use an air fryer baking pan. Working in batches if necessary, place the tomatoes and artichokes into the prepared basket and cook for 10 minutes.
4. When the tomatoes and artichokes are done, toss with the pasta and serve immediately.

Nutrition:
Calories: 187　　　　Carbs: 6g　　　　Sodium: 26mg
Fat: 8g　　　　Protein: 4g　　　　Potassium: 182.7mg

146. Black Bean Bake with Avocado

Preparation Time: 10 minutes Cooking time: 10 minutes Servings: 4

Ingredients:
- 1 or 15-ounce can low-sodium black beans, rinsed and drained
- 2 cups corn kernels (thawed, if frozen)
- 2 large bell peppers, diced
- 1/2 cup chopped red onion
- 1 garlic clove, minced
- 2 tablespoons extra-virgin olive oil
- 1 tablespoon freshly squeezed lime juice
- 2 teaspoons chili powder
- 2 teaspoons ground cumin
- 1/2 teaspoon paprika
- 1/4 teaspoon dried onion granules
- 1/4 teaspoon dried oregano
- 1 teaspoon freshly ground black pepper
- 3 tablespoons nutritional yeast
- 1 cup chopped fresh cilantro, for garnish
- 1 Hass avocado, sliced

Directions:
1. Preheat the air fryer to 375F.
2. In a bowl, set together the black beans, corn, bell peppers, onion, garlic, olive oil, lime juice, chili powder, cumin, paprika, onion, oregano, and pepper.
3. Working in batches if necessary, spread the bean mixture in an air fryer baking pan and bring the pan in the air fryer basket. Cook for 6 minutes.
4. After the timer goes off, sprinkle the mixture with the nutritional yeast and cook for another 3 minutes until the top is golden brown.
5. To serve, remove from the pan, garnish with the cilantro, and top with the avocado slices.

Nutrition:
Calories: 70 Fat: 0g Sodium: 6 mg
Carbs: 1/5g Protein: 2g Potassium: 121.6mg

147. Falafel with Mint-Tahini Sauce

Preparation Time: 15 minutes Cooking time: 10 minutes Servings: 4

Ingredients:
For the falafel
- 1 cup dried chickpeas, soaked overnight, drained, rinsed, and patted dry
- 1/2 red onion, chopped
- 1/2 red bell pepper, chopped
- 1/2 cup fresh parsley, stemmed
- 1/2 cup chopped fresh mint
- 1 teaspoon ground cumin
- 2 garlic cloves, minced
- 1/4 teaspoon dried oregano
- 1/4 teaspoon sea salt
- 1 teaspoon extra-virgin olive oil

For the mint-tahini sauce
- 1/2 cup tahini
- 1/2 cup chopped fresh mint
- 2 tablespoons freshly squeezed lemon juice
- 1/4 teaspoon sea salt
- 3 tablespoons water (optional)

Directions:
To make the falafel
1. Preheat the air fryer to 350F.
2. In a food processor bowl, merge the chickpeas, onion, bell pepper, parsley, mint, cumin, garlic, oregano, salt, and olive oil. Pulse, scraping down the bowl occasionally, until well combined into a rough paste.
3. Using damp hands, divide the falafel mixture into 10 patties, about 1 inch thick.
4. Working in batches if necessary, set the patties in a single layer in the air fryer basket. Set the temperature to 350F and process for 8 minutes, flipping halfway through, or until golden brown.

To make the mint-tahini sauce
1. While the falafel is cooking, in a medium bowl, stir together the tahini, mint, lemon juice, and salt until smooth. If the sauce is thick, add the water, 1 tablespoon at a time, until it reaches a consistency thin enough for dipping.
2. Serve the warm falafel with the mint-tahini sauce.

Nutrition:
Calories: 16　　　　　　　　　Carbs: 2.2 g　　　　　　　　　Sodium: 34 mg
Fat: 2 g　　　　　　　　　　　Protein: 11 g　　　　　　　　　Potassium: 116 mg

148. Quinoa-Lentil Burgers

Preparation Time: 20 minutes　　　Cooking time: 10 minutes　　　Servings: 4

Ingredients:
- 1/3cup dry quinoa
- 1 cup dried red lentils
- 4 cups water
- 4 cups spinach
- 2 ounces (12 to 15) sun-dried tomatoes, chopped
- 1/2 large red onion, chopped
- 1/2 cup almond flour
- 1/4 teaspoon granulated garlic
- 1/4 teaspoon ground cumin

Directions:
1. In a medium saucepan, merge the quinoa and lentils with the water. Set to a boil, then reduce the heat, cover, and simmer until the quinoa and lentils are cooked through, about 15 minutes. In the last minute of cooking, attach the spinach and let wilt.
2. Drain the quinoa mixture and transfer to a large bowl. Stir in the sun-dried tomatoes, onion, almond flour, garlic, and cumin then cover and refrigerate for at least 30 minutes.
3. Preheat the air fryer to 350F.
4. Divide the burger mixture into 4 large patties, about 5 inches in diameter.
5. Working in batches if necessary, place the burgers in a single layer in the air fryer basket and cook for 10 minutes. Flip the burgers over and process for another 2 minutes, or until golden brown. Serve immediately over salad or in a whole wheat bun.

Nutrition:
Calories: 164　　　　　　　　Carbs: 4.1g　　　　　　　　　Sodium: 39.5mg
Fat: 1g　　　　　　　　　　　Protein: 4g　　　　　　　　　　Potassium: 127.9mg

149. Eggplant Bites with Marinara

Preparation Time: 20 minutes　　　Cooking time: 10 minutes　　　Servings: 4

Ingredients:
For the marinara sauce
- 1 tablespoon extra-virgin olive oil
- 2 garlic cloves, minced
- 1 (15-ounce) can crushed tomatoes
- 1 tablespoon dried oregano
- 1 tablespoon dried basil
- 1/2 teaspoon freshly ground black pepper
- 1/2 teaspoon dried parsley

For the eggplant bites
- 1 medium eggplant, skinned and cut into cubes
- 1 cup unsweetened almond milk
- 1 tablespoon extra-virgin olive oil
- 2 cups whole wheat panko bread crumbs
- 1/4 cup nutritional yeast, plus more for sprinkling
- 1 tablespoon granulated garlic
- 1 tablespoon dried oregano
- 1/4 teaspoon sea salt
- Extra-virgin olive oil cooking spray

Directions:
To make the marinara sauce
1. In a saucepan over medium-low heat, warmth the olive oil, then add the garlic and sauté for 1 to 2 minutes, until fragrant.
2. Add the tomatoes, oregano, basil, pepper, and parsley. Simmer for 8 minutes, or until the sauce starts to bubble, stirring occasionally. Keep warm until ready to use.

To make the eggplant bites
1. Preheat the air fryer to 370°F.
2. Place the eggplant on a paper towel or dishcloth and allow moisture to drain for about 5 minutes, then pat dry.
3. In a bowl, set together the almond milk and olive oil. In another bowl, set together the panko bread crumbs, nutritional yeast, garlic, oregano, and salt.
4. One at a time, dunk the eggplant cubes into the almond milk mixture and then coat in the panko bread crumb mixture.
5. Working in batches if necessary, set the eggplant in a single layer in the air fryer basket. Mist with the olive oil and cook for 9 minutes, shaking or stirring halfway through.
6. After the timer goes off, sprinkle with additional nutritional yeast and cook for another 1 minute, until golden brown. Serve the eggplant bites with the marinara sauce on the side for dipping.

Nutrition:
Calories: 71
Fat: 4g
Carbs: 5g
Protein: 5g
Sodium: 35mg
Potassium: 148.2mg

150. Broccoli Salad

Preparation time: 10 minutes Cooking time: 15 minutes Servings: 6
Ingredients:
- 10 slices bacon
- 1 cup fresh broccoli
- 1/4 cup red onion, minced
- 1/2 cup raisins
- 3 tbsp. white wine vinegar
- 2 tbsp. white sugar
- 1 cup mayonnaise
- 1 cup sunflower seeds

Directions:
1. Cook the bacon in a deep-frying pan over medium heat. Drain, crumble, and set aside. Combine broccoli, onion, and raisins in a medium bowl. Mix vinegar, sugar, and mayonnaise in a small bowl. Pour over the broccoli mixture and mix. Cool for at least 2 hours.
2. Before serving, mix the salad with crumbled bacon and sunflower seeds.

Nutrition:
Calories: 91
Fat: 0g
Carbs: 5g
Protein: 1g
Sodium: 0mg
Potassium: 138.2mg

151. Kale, Quinoa, and Avocado Salad

Preparation time: 5 minutes Cooking time: 25 minutes Servings: 4
Ingredients:
- 2/3 cup quinoa
- 1 1/3 cup water
- 1 bunch kale, torn into bite-sized pieces
- 1/2 avocado, peeled, diced, and pitted
- 1/2 cup cucumber, chopped
- 1/3 cup red pepper, chopped
- 2 tbsp. red onion, chopped
- 1 tbsp. feta cheese, crumbled

Directions:
1. Boil the quinoa and 1 1/3 cup of water in a pan. Adjust heat and simmer until quinoa is tender and water is absorbed for about 15 to 20 minutes. Set aside to cool.

2. Place the cabbage in a steam basket over more than an inch of boiling water in a pan. Seal the pan with a lid and steam until hot, about 45 seconds; transfer to a large plate. Garnish with cabbage, quinoa, avocado, cucumber, pepper, red onion, and feta cheese.
3. Combine olive oil, lemon juice, Dijon mustard, sea salt, and black pepper in a bowl until the oil is emulsified in the dressing; pour over the salad.

Nutrition:
Calories: 149　　　　　Carbs: 3g　　　　　Sodium: 74 mg
Fat: 6g　　　　　Protein: 8g　　　　　Potassium: 150.5mg

152. Garden Salad

Preparation time: 5 minutes　　　Cooking time: 20 minutes　　　Servings: 6

Ingredients:
- 1 lb. raw peanuts in the shell
- 1 bay leaf
- 2 medium-sized tomatoes, chopped up
- 1/2 cup green pepper, diced up
- 1/2 cup sweet onion, diced up
- 1/4 cup hot pepper, finely diced
- 1/4 cup celery, diced up
- 2 tbsp. olive oil
- 3/4 tsp. flavored vinegar
- 1/4 tsp. black pepper, freshly ground

Directions:
1. Boil your peanuts for 1 minute and rinse them.
2. The skin will be soft, so discard the skin.
3. Attach 2 cups of water to the Instant Pot.
4. Add bay leaf and peanuts.
5. Lock the lid and cook on HIGH pressure for 20 minutes.
6. Drain the water.
7. Take a large bowl and add the peanuts, diced vegetables.
8. Whisk in olive oil, lemon juice, pepper in another bowl.
9. Spill the mixture over the salad and mix. Enjoy!

Nutrition:
Calories: 156　　　　　Carbs: 2.2 g　　　　　Sodium: 16 mg
Protein: 9.4 g　　　　　Fat: 7.1 g　　　　　Potassium: 165 mg

153. Baked Smoky Broccoli and Garlic

Preparation time: 5 minutes　　　Cooking time: 20 minutes　　　Servings: 6

Ingredients:
- Cooking spray
- 1 tbsp. extra-virgin olive oil
- 3 cloves garlic, minced
- 1/4 tsp. sea salt
- 1/4 tsp. black pepper, ground
- 1/2 tsp. cumin
- 1/2 tsp. annatto seeds
- 3 1/2 cups broccoli, sliced
- 1 lime, cut into wedges
- 1 tbsp. fresh cilantro, chopped

Directions:
1. Preheat your oven to 450F.
2. Set a baking sheet with foil and grease with olive oil.
3. Mix the olive oil, garlic, cumin, annatto seeds, salt, and pepper in a bowl.
4. Add in the cauliflower, carrots, and broccoli.
5. Combine until well coated.
6. Bring in a layer on the baking sheet.
7. Add the lime wedges.
8. Roast in the oven until vegetables become caramelized, for about 25 minutes.
9. Take out the lime wedges and top with the cilantro.

Nutrition:
Calories: 156　　　　　　　　　Carbs: 2.2 g　　　　　　　　　Sodium: 16 mg
Protein: 9.4 g　　　　　　　　　Fat: 7.1 g　　　　　　　　　　Potassium: 135 mg

154. Roasted Cauliflower and Lima Beans

Preparation time: 5 minutes　　　Cooking time: 20 minutes　　　Servings: 6

Ingredients:
- Cooking spray
- 1 tbsp. vegan butter/margarine, melted
- 9 cloves garlic, minced
- 1/4 tsp. sea salt
- 1/4 tsp. black pepper, ground
- 1 1/2 cups cauliflower, sliced
- 3 1/2 cups cherry tomatoes
- 1 (15 oz.) can lima beans, drained
- 1 lemon, cut into wedges

Directions:
1. Preheat your oven to 450F.
2. Set a baking sheet with foil and grease with melted vegan butter or margarine.
3. Mix the olive oil, garlic, salt, and pepper in a bowl.
4. Add in the cauliflower, tomatoes, and lima beans
5. Combine until well coated.
6. Set them out in a single layer on the baking sheet.
7. Add the lemon wedges.
8. Roast in the oven until vegetables become caramelized, for about 25 minutes.
9. Take out the lemon wedges.

Nutrition:
Calories: 156　　　　　　　　　Carbs: 12.2 g　　　　　　　　Sodium: 26 mg
Protein: 9.4 g　　　　　　　　　Fat: 7.1 g　　　　　　　　　　Potassium: 176 mg

155. Cauliflower Salad with Tahini Vinaigrette

Preparation time: 15 minutes　　Cooking time: 5 minutes　　　Servings: 2

Ingredients:
- 1 1/2 lb. cauliflower
- 1/4 cup cherries, dried
- 3 tbsp. lemon juice
- 1 tbsp. fresh mint, chopped
- 1 tsp. olive oil
- 1/2 cup parsley, chopped
- 3 tbsp. pistachios, roasted, salted, and chopped
- 1/4 tsp. salt
- 1/4 cup shallot, chopped
- 2 tbsp. tahini

Directions:
1. Grate the cauliflower in a microwave-safe container. Add olive oil and 1/4 salt. Be sure to cover and season the cauliflower evenly. Wrap the bowl with plastic wrap and heat it in the microwave for about 3 minutes.
2. Put the rice with the cauliflower on a baking sheet and let cool for about 10 minutes. Add the lemon juice and the shallots. Let it rest to allow the cauliflower to absorb the flavor.
3. Add the mixture of tahini, cherries, parsley, mint, and salt. Mix everything well. Sprinkle with roasted pistachios before serving.

Nutrition:
Calories: 185　　　　　　　　　Carbs: 1g　　　　　　　　　　Sodium: 5mg
Fat: 18g　　　　　　　　　　　Protein: 5g　　　　　　　　　　Potassium: 128.3mg

156. White Beans with Spinach and Pan-Roasted Tomatoes

Preparation time: 15 minutes Cooking time: 10 minutes Servings: 2

Ingredients:
- 1 tbsp. olive oil
- 4 small plum tomatoes, halved lengthwise
- 10 oz. spinach, frozen, defrosted and squeezed of excess water
- 2 garlic cloves, thinly sliced
- 2 tbsp. water
- 1/4 tsp. black pepper, freshly ground
- 1 can white beans, drained
- Juice of 1 lemon

Directions:
1. Warmth up the oil in a large skillet over medium-high heat. Put the tomatoes, cut-side down, and cook within 3 to 5 minutes; turn and cook within 1 minute more. Transfer to a plate.
2. Reduce heat to medium and add the spinach, garlic, water, and pepper to the skillet. Cook, tossing until the spinach is heated through, 2 to 3 minutes.
3. Return the tomatoes to the skillet, put the white beans and lemon juice, and toss until heated through 1 to 2 minutes.

Nutrition:
Calories: 214 Carbs: 2 g Sodium: 15 mg
Fat: 8 g Protein: 30 g Potassium: 121 mg

157. Bean Hummus

Preparation time: 10 minutes Cooking time: 40 minutes Servings: 6

Ingredients:
- 1 cup chickpeas, soaked
- 6 cups of water
- 1 tablespoon tahini paste
- 2 garlic cloves,
- 1/4 cup olive oil
- 1/4 cup lemon juice
- 1 teaspoon harissa

Directions:
1. Pour water into the saucepan. Add chickpeas and close the lid.
2. Cook the chickpeas for 40 minutes on low heat or until they are soft.
3. After this, transfer the cooked chickpeas to the food processor.
4. Add olive oil, harissa, lemon juice, garlic cloves, and tahini paste.
5. Blend the hummus until it is smooth.

Nutrition:
Calories: 209 Carbs: 2.2 g Sodium: 13 mg
Fat: 4 g Protein: 10 g Potassium: 127 mg

158. Hasselback Eggplant

Preparation time: 15 minutes Cooking time: 25 minutes Servings: 2

Ingredients:
- 2 eggplants, trimmed
- 2 tomatoes, sliced
- 1 tablespoon low-fat yogurt
- 1 teaspoon curry powder
- 1 teaspoon olive oil

Directions:
1. Make the cuts in the eggplant in the shape of Hasselback.
2. Then spread the vegetables with curry powder and fill with sliced tomatoes.
3. Drizzle the eggplants with olive oil and yogurt and wrap them in the foil (each Hasselback eggplant wrap separately).
4. Process the vegetables at 375F for 25 minutes.

Nutrition:
Calories: 297 Carbs: 2 g Sodium: 26 mg
Fat: 9 g Protein: 20 g Potassium: 187 mg

159. Black-Eyed Peas and Greens Power Salad

Preparation time: 15 minutes Cooking time: 6 minutes Servings: 2

Ingredients:
- 1 tbsp. olive oil
- 3 cups purple cabbage, chopped
- 5 cups baby spinach
- 1 cup carrots, shredded
- 1 can black-eyed peas, drained
- Juice of 1/2 lemon
- 1/4 tsp. Salt
- Black pepper, freshly ground

Directions:
1. In a medium pan, add the oil and cabbage and sauté for 1 to 2 minutes on medium heat. Add in your spinach, cover for 3 to 4 minutes on medium heat, until greens are wilted. Remove from the heat and add to a large bowl.
2. Add in the carrots, black-eyed peas, and a splash of lemon juice. Season with salt and pepper, if desired. Toss and serve.

Nutrition:
Calories: 97 Carbs: 8 g Sodium: 23 mg
Fat: 4 g Protein: 4 g Potassium: 127 mg

160. Butternut-Squash Macaroni and Cheese

Preparation time: 15 minutes Cooking time: 20 minutes Servings: 2

Ingredients:
- 1 cup whole-wheat ziti macaroni
- 2 cups butternut squash, peeled and cubed
- 1 cup non-fat or low-fat milk, divided
- Black pepper, freshly ground
- 1 tsp. Dijon mustard
- 1 tbsp. olive oil
- 1/4 cup low-fat cheddar cheese, shredded

Directions:
1. Cook the pasta al dente. Put the butternut squash plus 1/2 cup milk in a medium saucepan and place over medium-high heat. Season with black pepper. Bring it to a simmer. Lower the heat, then cook until fork-tender, 8 to 10 minutes.
2. To a blender, add squash and Dijon mustard. Purée until smooth. Meanwhile, set a sauté pan and add olive oil. Add the squash purée and the remaining 1/2 cup of milk. Simmer within 5 minutes. Add the cheese and stir to combine.
3. Add the pasta to the sauté pan and stir to combine. Serve immediately.

Nutrition:
Calories: 107 Carbs: 1.1 g Sodium: 49 mg
Fat: 2 g Protein: 6 g Potassium: 161 mg

161. Healthy Vegetable Fried Rice

Preparation time: 15 minutes Cooking time: 10 minutes Servings: 4

Ingredients:
For the sauce:
- 1/3 cup garlic vinegar
- 1 1/2 tbsp. dark molasses
- 1 tsp. onion powder

For the fried rice:
- 1 tsp. olive oil
- 2 whole eggs, slightly beaten + 4 egg whites

- 1 cup mixed vegetables, frozen
- 1 cup Edamame, frozen
- 2 cups brown rice, cooked

Directions:
1. Prepare the sauce by combining the garlic vinegar, molasses, and onion powder in a glass jar. Shake well.
2. Warmth up the oil in a large wok or skillet over medium-high heat. Add eggs and egg whites, let cook until the eggs set, for about 1 minute.
3. Break up eggs with a spatula or spoon into small pieces. Add frozen mixed vegetables and frozen edamame. Cook for 4 minutes, stirring frequently.
4. Add the brown rice and sauce to the vegetable-and-egg mixture. Cook for 5 minutes or until heated through. Serve immediately.

Nutrition:
Calories: 307
Fat: 9 g
Carbs: 1.8 g
Protein: 22 g
Sodium: 49 mg
Potassium: 161 mg

162. Carrot Cakes

Preparation time: 10 minutes   Cooking time: 10 minutes   Servings: 4

Ingredients:
- 1 cup carrot, grated
- 1 tablespoon semolina
- 1 egg, beaten
- 1 teaspoon Italian seasonings
- 1 tablespoon sesame oil

Directions:
1. In the bowl, mix up grated carrot, semolina, egg, and Italian seasonings.
2. Heat sesame oil in the skillet.
3. Make the carrot cakes with 2 spoons and put them in the skillet.
4. Cook the cakes for 4 minutes per side.

Nutrition:
Calories: 257
Fat: 7 g
Carbs: 2 g
Protein: 7 g
Sodium: 29 mg
Potassium: 161 mg

163. Vegan Chili

Preparation time: 10 minutes   Cooking time: 25 minutes   Servings: 4

Ingredients:
- 1/2 cup bulgur
- 1 cup tomatoes, chopped
- 1 chili pepper, chopped
- 1 cup red kidney beans, cooked
- 2 cups low-sodium vegetable broth
- 1 teaspoon tomato paste
- 1/2 cup celery stalk, chopped

Directions:
1. Put all ingredients in the big skillet and stir well.
2. Cover and simmer the chili for 25 minutes over medium-low heat.

Nutrition:
Calories: 16
Fat: 2 g
Carbs: 2.2 g
Protein: 11 g
Sodium: 34 mg
Potassium: 116 mg

164. Aromatic Whole Grain Spaghetti

Preparation time: 5 minutes   Cooking time: 10 minutes   Servings: 2

Ingredients:
- 1 teaspoon dried basil
- 1/4 cup of soy milk
- 6 oz. whole-grain spaghetti
- 2 cups of water

- 1 teaspoon ground nutmeg

Directions:
1. Set the water to boil, then add spaghetti and cook them for 8-10 minutes.
2. Meanwhile, bring the soy milk to boil.
3. Drain the cooked pasta and mix them up with ground nutmeg, soy milk and dried basil.
4. Stir the meal well.

Nutrition:
Calories: 177 Carbs: 2.5 g Sodium: 18 mg
Fat: 2 g Protein: 8 g Potassium: 110 mg

165. Chunky Tomatoes

Preparation time: 5 minutes Cooking time: 15 minutes Servings: 3

Ingredients:
- 2 cups plum tomatoes, roughly chopped
- 1/2 cup onion, diced
- 1/2 teaspoon garlic, diced
- 1 teaspoon Italian seasonings
- 1 teaspoon canola oil
- 1 chili pepper, chopped

Directions:
1. Heat canola oil in the saucepan.
2. Add chili pepper and onion. Cook the vegetables for 5 minutes. Stir them from time to time.
3. Then, add tomatoes, garlic, and Italian seasonings.
4. Cover and sauté the meal for 10 minutes.

Nutrition:
Calories: 77 Carbs: 7 g Sodium: 17 mg
Fat: 1 g Protein: 2 g Potassium: 276 mg

166. Baby minted carrots

Preparation time: 35 minutes Cooking time: 20 minutes Servings: 6

Ingredients:
- 6 cups of water
- 1-pound baby carrots, rinsed (about 5 1/2 cups)
- 1/4 cup 100% apple juice
- 1 tablespoon cornstarch
- 1/2 tablespoon chopped fresh mint leaves
- 1/8 teaspoon ground cinnamon

Directions:
1. Through a large bowl, pour the water. Attach the carrots and simmer for about 10 minutes, until tender-crisp. Drain the carrots in a serving bowl and set them aside.
2. Combine the apple juice and cornstarch in a shallow saucepan over moderate heat. Stir for about 5 minutes before the mixture thickens. Stir in the cinnamon and mint.
3. Pour over the carrots with the combination. Immediately serve.

Nutrition:
Calories: 47 Carbs: 1 g Sodium: 17 mg
Fat: 4 g Protein: 2 g Potassium: 146 mg

167. Baked Falafel

Preparation time: 10 minutes Cooking time: 25 minutes Servings: 6

Ingredients:
- 2 cups chickpeas, cooked
- 1 yellow onion, diced
- 3 tablespoons olive oil
- 1 cup fresh parsley, chopped
- 1 teaspoon ground cumin
- 1/2 teaspoon coriander
- 2 garlic cloves, diced

Directions:
1. Spill all ingredients in the blender and blend until smooth.
2. Preheat the oven to 375F.
3. Then line the baking sheet with baking paper.
4. Make balls with the chickpea mixture and gently press them into a falafel shape.
5. Put the falafel in the pan and bake in the oven for 25 minutes.

Nutrition:
Calories: 42   Carbs: 8 g   Sodium: 7 mg
Fat: 1 g   Protein: 2 g   Potassium: 56 mg

168. Paella

Preparation time: 10 min   Cooking time: 25 min   Servings: 6

Ingredients:
- 1 teaspoon dried saffron
- 1 cup short-grain rice
- 1 tablespoon olive oil
- 2 cups of water
- 1 teaspoon chili flakes
- 6 oz. artichoke hearts, chopped
- 1/2 cup green peas
- 1 onion, sliced
- 1 cup bell pepper, sliced

Directions:
1. Pour water into the saucepan. Add rice and cook it for 15 mins.
2. Meanwhile, heat olive oil in the skillet.
3. Add chili flakes, dried saffron, onion, and bell pepper.
4. Roast the vegetables for 5 minutes.
5. Add them to the cooked rice.
6. Then add green peas and artichoke hearts. Toss the paella well and cook it for 10 minutes over low heat.

Nutrition:
Calories: 252   Carbs: 15 g   Sodium: 15 mg
Fat: 7 g   Protein: 12 g   Potassium: 254 mg

169. Mushroom Cakes

Preparation time: 15 minutes   Cooking time: 10 minutes   Servings: 4

Ingredients:
- 2 cups mushrooms, chopped
- 3 garlic cloves, chopped
- 1 tablespoon dried dill
- 1 egg, beaten
- 1/4 cup of rice, cooked
- 1 tablespoon sesame oil
- 1 teaspoon chili powder

Directions:
1. Grind the mushrooms in the food processor.
2. Add egg, rice, garlic, dill and chili powder.
3. Blend the mixture for 10 seconds.
4. Then, heat up sesame oil for 1 minute.
5. Make the medium-sized mushroom cakes and put them in the hot sesame oil.
6. Cook the mushroom cakes for 10 minutes (about 5 minutes per side) on medium heat.

Nutrition:
Calories: 210   Carbs: 1.2 g   Sodium: 15 mg
Fat: 11 g   Protein: 8 g   Potassium: 154 mg

170. Glazed Eggplant Rings

Preparation time: 10 minutes Cooking time: 10 minutes Servings: 4

Ingredients:
- 3 eggplants, sliced
- 1 tablespoon liquid honey
- 1 teaspoon minced ginger
- 2 tablespoons lemon juice
- 3 tablespoons avocado oil
- 1/2 teaspoon ground coriander
- 3 tablespoons water

Directions:
1. Rub the eggplants with ground coriander.
2. Then heat the avocado oil in the skillet for 1 minute.
3. When the oil is very hot, add the sliced eggplant and arrange it in one layer.
4. Cook the vegetables for 2 minute per side.
5. Transfer the eggplant to the bowl.
6. Then add liquid honey, minced ginger, lemon juice, and water in the skillet.
7. Set it to a boil and then add cooked eggplants.
8. Cover the vegetables in the sweet liquid well and cook for another 2 minutes.

Nutrition:
Calories: 180 Carbs: 1.1 g Sodium: 25 mg
Fat: 8 g Protein: 3 g Potassium: 378 mg

171. Sweet Potato Balls

Preparation time: 15 minutes Cooking time: 10 minutes Servings: 4

Ingredients:
- 1 cup sweet potato, mashed, cooked
- 1 tablespoon fresh cilantro, chopped
- 1 egg, beaten
- 3 tablespoons ground oatmeal
- 1 teaspoon ground paprika
- 1/2 teaspoon ground turmeric
- 2 tablespoons coconut oil

Directions:
1. Mix up mashed sweet potato, paprika, fresh cilantro, egg, ground oatmeal, and turmeric in the bowl.
2. Toss the mixture until smooth and make the small balls.
3. Heat the coconut oil in the saucepan.
4. When the coconut oil is very hot, add the sweet potato balls.
5. Cook them until golden brown.

Nutrition:
Calories: 110 Carbs: 1.9 g Sodium: 25 mg
Fat: 0 g Protein: 2 g Potassium: 172 mg

172. Chickpea Curry

Preparation time: 10 minutes Cooking time: 10 minutes Servings: 4

Ingredients:
- 1 1/2 cup chickpeas, boiled
- 1 teaspoon curry powder
- 1/2 teaspoon garam masala
- 1 cup spinach, chopped
- 1 teaspoon coconut oil
- 1/4 cup of soy milk
- 1 tablespoon tomato paste
- 1/2 cup of water

Directions:
1. Heat coconut oil in the saucepan.
2. Add tomato paste, curry powder, garam masala and soy milk.
3. Toss the mixture until smooth and bring it to a boil.
4. Add water, spinach, and chickpeas.

5. Stir the meal and close the lid.
6. Cook it for 5 minutes over medium-high heat.

Nutrition:

Calories: 170 Carbs: 2.2 g Sodium: 24 mg
Fat: 5 g Protein: 6 g Potassium: 277 mg

173. Quinoa Bowl

Preparation time: 15 minutes Cooking time: 15 minutes Servings: 4

Ingredients:
- 1 cup quinoa
- 2 cups of water
- 1 cup tomatoes, diced
- 1 cup sweet pepper, diced
- 1/2 cup of rice, cooked
- 1 tablespoon lemon juice
- 1/2 teaspoon lemon zest, grated
- 1 tablespoon olive oil

Directions:
1. Mix up quinoa and water and cook it for 15 minutes. After this, remove it from the heat and leave it to rest for 10 minutes.
2. Transfer the cooked quinoa to the big bowl.
3. Add tomatoes, rice, lemon juice, sweet pepper, lemon zest, and olive oil.
4. Merge the mixture well and transfer it to the serving bowls.

Nutrition:

Calories: 200 Carbs: 2.4 g Sodium: 34 mg
Fat: 10 g Protein: 16 g Potassium: 175 mg

174. Vegan Meatloaf

Preparation time: 10 minutes Cooking time: 30 minutes Servings: 6

Ingredients:
- 1 cup chickpeas, cooked
- 1 onion, diced
- 1 tablespoon ground flax seeds
- 1/2 teaspoon chili flakes
- 1 tablespoon coconut oil
- 1/2 cup carrot, diced
- 1/2 cup celery stalk, chopped
- 1 tablespoon tomato paste

Directions:
1. Heat coconut oil in the saucepan.
2. Add onion, carrot and celery stalk. Cook the vegetables for 10 minutes.
3. Then add chili flakes, chickpeas and ground flax seeds.
4. Blend the mixture until smooth with the immersion blender.
5. After this, line the loaf mold with baking paper and transfer the blended mixture inside.
6. Flatten well and spread with tomato paste.
7. Bake the meatloaf in the preheated to 365°F oven for 22 minutes.

Nutrition:

Calories: 180 Carbs: 1.9 g Sodium: 30 mg
Fat: 5 g Protein: 15 g Potassium: 178 mg

175. Loaded Potato Skins

Preparation time: 15 minutes Cooking time: 45 minutes Servings: 6

Ingredients:
- 6 potatoes
- 1 teaspoon ground black pepper
- 2 tablespoons olive oil
- 1/2 teaspoon minced garlic
- 1/4 cup of soy milk

Directions:
1. Preheat the oven to 400F.
2. Tickle the potatoes with the help of the fork 2-3 times and bake for 30 minutes or until vegetables are tender.
3. After this, cut the baked potatoes into halves and scoop out the potato meat in the bowl.
4. Drizzle the scooped potato halves with olive oil and ground black pepper and return to the oven. Bake them until they are light brown.
5. Then, mash the scooped potato meat and mix it up with soy milk and minced garlic.
6. Fill the cooked potato halves with mashed potato mixture.

Nutrition:
Calories: 170
Fat: 8 g
Carbs: 1.4 g
Protein: 10 g
Sodium: 51 mg
Potassium: 108 mg

Chapter 8. Desserts

176. Banana-Cashew Cream Mousse

Preparation time: 55 minutes   Cooking time: 0 minutes   Servings: 2

Ingredients:

- 1/2 cup cashews, presoaked
- 1 tablespoon honey
- 1 teaspoon vanilla extract
- 1 large banana, sliced (reserve 4 slices for garnish)
- 1 cup plain nonfat Greek yogurt

Directions:
1. Set the cashews in a small bowl and cover with 1 cup of water.
2. Soak at room temperature for 2 to 3 hours.
3. Drain, rinse, and set aside.
4. Place honey, vanilla extract, cashews, and bananas in a blender or food processor.
5. Blend until smooth.
6. Place mixture in a medium bowl.
7. Fold in yogurt, mix well. Cover.
8. Chill in refrigerator, covered, for at least 45 minutes.
9. Portion mousse into 2 serving bowls. Garnish each with 2 banana slices.

Nutrition:

Calories: 329   Carbs: 1.4g   Sodium: 64mg
Fat: 14g   Protein: 17g   Potassium: 107mg

177. Cherry Stew

Preparation time: 10 minutes   Cooking time: 10 minutes   Servings: 6

Ingredients:

- 1/2 cup cocoa powder
- 1 lb. cherries, pitted
- 1/4 cup coconut sugar
- 2 cups water

Directions:
1. In a pan, combine the cherries with the water, sugar, and cocoa powder, stir, cook over medium heat for 10 minutes, divide into bowls and serve cold.
2. Enjoy!

Nutrition:

Calories: 214   Carbs: 2 g   Sodium: 15 mg
Fat: 8 g   Protein: 30 g   Potassium: 121 mg

178. Sriracha Parsnip Fries

Preparation time: 10 minutes   Cooking time: 25 minutes   Servings: 4

Ingredients:

- 1-pound parsnips, peeled, cut into 3 × 1/2-inch strips
- 1 tablespoon olive oil
- 1 teaspoon dried rosemary
- Sriracha to taste
- 1/2tsp. Salt and pepper to taste

Directions:
1. Preheat oven to 450F. Mix parsnips, rosemary, and oil in a medium size bowl.
2. Season with salt, pepper, and sriracha to taste and toss to coat.
3. Lay parsnips on a baking sheet making sure the strips don't overlap. (If they are touching, they will become mushy instead of crispy.) Bake for 10 minutes.
4. Turn and roast until parsnips are browned in spots, 10 to 15 minutes longer.
5. If you want them to be extra crispy, turn the broiler on for the last 2 to 3 minutes.

6. Remove from oven and enjoy.

Nutrition:
Calories 115　　　　　　　　　　Carbs 17 g　　　　　　　　　　Sodium 16 mg
Fat 2 g　　　　　　　　　　　　Protein 7 g　　　　　　　　　　Potassium 128 mg

179. Tortilla Strawberry Chips

Preparation time: 10 minutes　　　Cooking time: 25 minutes　　　Servings: 6

Ingredients:
- 15 strawberries
- 1/4 tsp. cayenne
- 2 tbsps. organic extra virgin olive oil
- 12 whole wheat grain tortillas
- 1 tbsp. chili powder

Directions:
1. Spread the tortillas for the lined baking sheet, add the oil, chili powder, strawberry and cayenne, toss, introduce inside oven and bake at 350F for 25 minutes.
2. Divide into bowls and serve as a side dish.
3. Enjoy!

Nutrition:
Calories: 209　　　　　　　　　　Carbs: 3.2 g　　　　　　　　　Sodium: 25 mg
Fat: 4 g　　　　　　　　　　　　Protein: 3 g　　　　　　　　　Potassium: 50 mg

180. Almond Rice Pudding

Preparation time: 10 minutes　　　Cooking time: 30 minutes　　　Servings: 3-4

Ingredients:
- 1/4 cup sugar
- 1 tsp. vanilla
- 3 cup milk
- 1 cup white rice
- 1/4 c. toasted almonds
- Cinnamon, as required
- 1/4 tsp. almond extract

Directions:
1. Get the milk and rice together in a pan and boil and simmer it by lowering the heat for half an hour with the top on till the rice softens up a bit.
2. Take it off the burner and put in sugar, almond, vanilla and cinnamon.
3. Garish roasted almonds at the top and eat it warm.

Nutrition:
Calories: 257　　　　　　　　　　Carbs: 2 g　　　　　　　　　　Sodium: 29 mg
Fat: 7 g　　　　　　　　　　　　Protein: 7 g　　　　　　　　　Potassium: 161 mg

181. Sweet Potatoes and Apples Mix

Preparation Time: 10 minutes　　　Cooking Time: 1 hour and 10 minutes　　　Servings: 1

Ingredients:
- 1 tbsp. low-fat butter
- 1/2 lb. cored and chopped apples
- 2 tbsp. water
- 2 lbs. sweet potatoes

Directions:
1. Arrange the potatoes around the lined baking sheet, bake inside oven at 400 0F for an hour, peel them and mash them in the meat processor.
2. Put apples in the very pot, add the river, bring using a boil over medium heat, reduce temperature, and cook for ten minutes.
3. Transfer to your bowl, add mashed potatoes, stir well and serve every day.

4. Enjoy!

Nutrition:
Calories: 252　　　　　　　Carbs: 15 g　　　　　　　　Sodium: 15 mg
Fat: 7 g　　　　　　　　　 Protein: 12 g　　　　　　　 Potassium: 254 mg

182. Sautéed Bananas with Orange Sauce

Preparation time: 5 minutes　　Cooking time: 5 minutes　　Servings: 4

Ingredients:
- 1/4 cup frozen pure orange juice concentrate
- 2 tbsp. margarine
- 1/4 cup sliced almonds
- 1 tsp. orange zest
- 1 tsp. fresh grated ginger
- 4 firm, sliced ripe bananas
- 1 tsp. cinnamon

Directions:
1. Dissolve the margarine over medium heat in a large skillet, until it bubbles but before it begins to brown.
2. Add the cinnamon, ginger, and orange zest. Cook, while stirring, for 1 minute before adding the orange juice concentrate.
3. Cook, while stirring until an even sauce has formed.
4. Add the bananas and cook, stirring carefully for 1-2 minutes, or until warmed and evenly coated with the sauce.
5. Serve warm with sliced almonds.

Nutrition:
Calories: 135　　　　　　　Carbs: 2.6 g　　　　　　　 Sodium: 16 mg
Fat: 2 g　　　　　　　　　 Protein: 5 g　　　　　　　　Potassium: 157 mg

183. Caramelized Blood Oranges with Ginger Cream

Preparation time: 10 minutes　　Cooking time: 15 minutes　　Servings: 4

Ingredients:
- 2 tbsp. low sugar orange marmalade
- 1 tbsp. divided fresh grated ginger
- 4 c. peeled and sliced blood oranges
- 2 tbsp. brown sugar
- Candied orange peel
- 1/2 cup coconut cream

Directions:
1. Begin by preheating the broiler.
2. In a small saucepan merge the orange marmalade and two teaspoons of the fresh ginger. Heat over low heat and stir until the mixture becomes slightly liquefied.
3. Place a thin layer of the oranges into the bottom of four large baking ramekins and then brush with the marmalade mixture. Repeat this step until all of the oranges have been used. Pour any remaining gingered marmalade over the tops of the ramekins.
4. Sprinkle each ramekin with brown sugar and place under the broiler for approximately 5 minutes, or until caramelized.
5. Serve warm garnished with coconut cream and candied orange peel, if desired.
6. To make the coconut cream: Take one can of pure, unsweetened coconut milk and place it in your refrigerator for 24 hours. Set the can out of the refrigerator and scoop out the thick cream that has settled on top. Place this in a bowl, along with one teaspoon of ginger and beat until creamy.

Nutrition:
Calories: 156　　　　　　　Carbs: 12.2 g　　　　　　　Sodium: 26 mg
Protein: 9.4 g　　　　　　　Fat: 7.1 g　　　　　　　　 Potassium: 176 mg

184. Grilled Minted Watermelon

Preparation time: 10 minutes Cooking time: 10 minutes Servings: 4

Ingredients:
- 1 tbsp. honey
- 1/4 c. finely chopped fresh mint
- 8 thick deseeded watermelon slices

Directions:
1. Prepare and preheat a stovetop grill.
2. Lightly press towels against the watermelon slices to remove as much excess moisture as possible.
3. Lightly brush both sides of the watermelon slices with honey.
4. Place the watermelon slices on the grill and grill for approximately 3 minutes per side, or until slightly caramelized.
5. Serve warm, sprinkled with fresh mint.

Nutrition:
Calories: 214 Carbs: 7.7g Sodium: 16.6mg
Protein: 2.6g Fat: 19.8 Potassium: 232mg

185. Caramelized Apricot Pots

Preparation time: 10 minutes Cooking time: 5 minutes Servings: 6

Ingredients:
- 1/4 cup white sugar
- 2 tsps. lemon juice
- 1/2 tsp. thyme
- 3 cup sliced apricots
- 1 tbsp. brown sugar
- 1 cup part skim ricotta cheese
- 1 tsp. lemon zest

Directions:
1. Preheat the broiler of your oven.
2. Place the apricots in a bowl and toss with the lemon juice.
3. In another bowl, combine the ricotta cheese, thyme, and lemon zest. Mix well.
4. Spread a layer of the ricotta mixture into the bottoms of 6 large baking ramekins.
5. Spoon the apricots over the top of the ricotta cheese in each.
6. Combine the white sugar and brown sugar. Sprinkle evenly over the apricots, avoiding large clumps of sugar as much as possible.
7. Place the ramekins under the broiler for approximately 5 minutes, or until caramelized.
8. Serve warm.

Nutrition:
Calories: 361 Carbs: 2.8g Protein: 9g
Fat: 16g Sodium: 55mg Potassium: 132mg

186. Pumpkin Pie

Preparation time: 15 minutes Cooking time: 45 minutes Servings: 8

Ingredients:
- 1 cup ginger cookies
- 1 can (15 oz.) pumpkin, pureed
- 1/2 cup egg whites
- 1/2 cup sugar
- 2 teaspoons pumpkin pie spice
- 1 can (12 oz.) evaporated skim milk
- 1 teaspoon ground cinnamon
- 1/2 teaspoon ground ginger
- 1/2 teaspoon ground nutmeg

Directions:
1. Add cookies to a food processor and blitz until coarsely chopped.
2. Preheat the oven to 35°F and coat a springform pan with cooking spray.
3. Spread the crumbled cookies onto the bottom of the pan and press into the bottom.

4. Mix pumpkin, egg whites, sugar, milk, pumpkin pie spice, cinnamon, ginger, and nutmeg in a bowl.
5. Spill the mixture on the crust and bake for 45 minutes.
6. Let cool slightly before serving.

Nutrition:
Calories: 304   Sodium: 56mg   Protein: 28g
Fat: 12g   Carbs: 3g   Potassium: 187mg

187. Chocolate Avocado Mousse

Preparation time: 5 minutes + chilling time
Cooking time: 5 minutes
Servings: 4

Ingredients:
- 1 avocado
- 1/4 cup almond milk
- 1/4 cup cacao powder
- 1 teaspoon vanilla extract
- 2 tablespoons coconut oil

Directions:
1. Attach all ingredients to a blender and blitz until smooth.
2. Divide the mixture among ramekins, cover and refrigerate for at least 1-2 hours.
3. Serve.

Nutrition:
Calories: 124   Protein: 3g   Sodium: 0mg
Carbs: 3g   Fat: 13g   Potassium: 142mg

188. Lemon Cheesecake

Preparation time: 5 minutes + chilling time
Cooking time: 10 minutes
Servings: 8

Ingredients:
- 2 cups low fat cottage cheese;
- 1/2 cup skim milk;
- 2 egg whites;
- 1/4 cup sugar;
- 1 teaspoon vanilla;
- 2 tablespoons cold water;
- 1 envelope gelatin, unflavored;
- 2 tablespoon lemon juice.

Directions:
1. Mix water, gelatin, and lemon juice in a bowl.
2. Let rest until gelatin softens. Add milk to a saucepan and heat until almost boiling.
3. Add gelatin powder and stir until dissolved. Add egg whites, vanilla, sugar, and cottage cheese.
4. Attach the mixture to a blender and process until smooth.
5. Pour the batter into a baking dish and refrigerate for 2-3 minutes.
6. Serve topped with lemon zest.

Nutrition:
Calories: 466   Carbs: 5.4g   Sodium: 16.2mg
Protein: 28.7g   Fat: 21.1g   Potassium: 112mg

189. Apple and Almond Muffins

Preparation time: 10 minutes
Cooking time: 20 minutes
Servings: 6

Ingredients:
- 6 ounces ground almonds
- 1 teaspoon cinnamon
- 1/2 teaspoon baking powder
- 1 pinch sunflower seed
- 1 whole egg
- 1 teaspoon apple cider vinegar
- 2 tablespoons Erythritol
- 1/3 cup apple sauce

Directions:
1. Pre-heat your oven to 350F. Set muffin tin with paper muffin cups, keep them on the side.
2. Merge in almonds, cinnamon, baking powder, sunflower seeds and keep it on the side. Set another bowl and beat in eggs, apple cider vinegar, apple sauce, Erythritol.
3. Attach the mix to dry ingredients and mix well until you have a smooth batter. Spill batter into tin and bake for 20 minutes. Once processed, let them cool. Serve and enjoy!

Nutrition:
Calories: 40 Carbs: 5 g Sodium: 150 mg
Fat: 1 g Protein: 3 g Potassium: 220 mg

190. Toasted Almond Ambrosia

Preparation time: 10 minutes Cooking time: 20 minutes Servings: 2

Ingredients:
- 1/2 cup almonds, slivered
- 1/2 cup coconut, shredded and unsweetened
- 3 cups pineapple, cubed
- 5 oranges, segment
- 2 red apples, cored and diced
- 2 tablespoons cream sherry
- mint leaves, fresh to garnish
- 1 banana, halved lengthwise, peeled and sliced

Directions:
1. Start by heating your oven to 325, and then get out a baking sheet.
2. Roast your almonds for ten minutes, making sure they're spread out evenly.
3. Transfer them to a plate and then toast your coconut on the same baking sheet.
4. Toast for ten minutes. Mix your banana, sherry, oranges, apples and pineapple in a bowl.
5. Divide the mixture not serving bowls and top with coconut and almonds. Garnish with mint before serving.

Nutrition:
Calories: 187 Carbs: 6g Sodium: 26mg
Fat: 8g Protein: 4g Potassium: 182.7mg

191. Key Lime Cherry "Nice" Cream

Preparation time: 10 minutes Cooking time: 15 minutes Servings: 4

Ingredients:
- 4 frozen bananas, peeled
- 1 cup frozen dark sweet cherries
- Zest and juice of 1 lime, divided
- 1/2 teaspoon vanilla extract
- 1/4 teaspoon kosher or sea salt

Directions:
1. Simply merge the ingredients in a food processor and enjoy a frozen treat.
2. Place the bananas, cherries, lime juice, vanilla extract, and salt in a food processor and purée until smooth, scraping the sides as needed.
3. Transfer the "nice" cream to bowls and top with the lime zest.
4. For leftovers, place the "nice" cream in airtight containers and store in the freezer for up to 1 month.
5. Let thaw for 30 minutes, until it reaches a soft-serve ice cream texture.

Nutrition:
Calories: 149 Carbs: 3g Sodium: 74 mg
Fat: 6g Protein: 8g Potassium: 150.5mg

192. Tart Raspberry Crumble Bar

Preparation time: 10 minutes Cooking time: 45 minutes Servings: 9

Ingredients:
- 1/2 cup whole toasted almonds
- 1 3/4 cup whole wheat flour
- 1/4 teaspoon salt
- 1/2 cup granulated sugar
- 18-ounce fresh raspberries
- 3/4 cup cold, unsalted butter, sliced into cubes
- 3 tablespoons cold water, or more if needed

Directions:
1. In a food processor, pulse almonds until copped coarsely.
2. Transfer to a bowl. Add flour and salt into food processor and pulse until a bit combined.
3. Attach butter and pulse until you have a coarse batter.
4. Evenly divide batter into two bowls. In first bowl of batter, knead well until it forms a ball.
5. Wrap in cling wrap, flatten a bit and chill for an hour for easy handling.
6. In second bowl of batter, add sugar. In a pinching motion, pinch batter to form clusters of streusels. Set aside.
7. When ready to bake, warmth oven to 375°F and lightly grease an 8x8-inch baking pan with cooking spray.
8. Discard cling wrap and evenly press dough on bottom of pan, up to 1-inch up the sides of the pan, making sure that everything is covered in dough.
9. Evenly spread raspberries. Top with streusel.
10. Pop in the oven and process until golden brown and berries are bubbly, around 45 minutes.
11. Detach from oven and cool for 20 minutes before slicing into 9 equal bars.
12. Serve and enjoy or store in a lidded container for 10-days in the fridge.

Nutrition:
Calories: 447 Carbs: 3g Sodium: 67mg
Protein: 37g Fat: 21.8g Potassium: 187mg

193. Easy Coconut-Carrot Cake Balls

Preparation time: 10 minutes Cooking time: 0 minutes Servings: 16

Ingredients:
- 3/4 cup peeled and finely shredded carrot
- 1 cup packed pitted medjool dates
- 1 3/4 cups raw walnuts
- 3/4 tsp. ground cinnamon
- 1/2 tsp. ground ginger
- 1 pinch ground nutmeg
- 2 tsp. vanilla extract
- 5 tbsp. almond flour
- 1/4 cup raisins
- 1/4 cup desiccated coconut flakes

Directions:
1. In food processor, process dates until it clumps.
2. Transfer to a bowl. In same food processor, process walnuts, cinnamon, ginger, and nutmeg. Process until it resembles a fine meal.
3. Add the processed dates, extract, almond flour, and shredded carrots.
4. Pulse until you form a loose dough but not mushy. Do not over-pulse.
5. Transfer to a bowl. Pulse desiccated coconut into tinier flakes and transfer to a small plate.
6. Divide the carrot batter into 4 and then divide each part into 4 to make a total of 16 equal sized balls.
7. Roll the balls in the coconut flakes, set in a lidded contained, and refrigerate for 2 hours before enjoying.

Nutrition:
Calories: 214 Carbs: 7.7g Sodium: 16.6mg
Protein: 2.6g Fat: 19.8 Potassium: 232mg

194. Apple Dumplings

Preparation Time: 10 minutes Cooking Time: 30 minutes Servings: 4

Ingredients:

Dough:
- 1 tablespoon butter
- 1 teaspoon honey, raw
- 1 cup whole wheat flour
- 2 tablespoons buckwheat flour
- 2 tablespoons rolled oats
- 2 tablespoons brandy or apple liquor

Filling:
- 2 tablespoons honey, raw
- 1 teaspoon nutmeg
- 6 tart apples, sliced thin
- 1 lemon, zested

Directions:
1. Turn the oven to 350.
2. Get out a food processor and mix your butter, flours, honey and oats until it forms a crumbly mixture.
3. Add in your brandy or apple liquor, pulsing until it forms a dough.
4. Seal in a plastic and place it in the fridge for two hours.
5. Toss your apples in lemon zest, honey and nutmeg.
6. Roll your dough into a sheet that's a quarter inch thick. Cut out eight-inch circles, placing each circle into a muffin tray that's been greased.
7. Press the dough down and then stuff with the apple mixture. Fold the edges, and pinch them closed. Make sure that they're well sealed.
8. Bake for a half hour until golden brown, and serve drizzled in honey.

Nutrition:

Calories: 159 Carbs: 2.4 g Sodium: 6 mg
Protein: 3 g Fat: 3.9 g Potassium: 325mg

195. Cauliflower Cinnamon Pudding

Preparation time: 10 minutes Cooking time: 20 minutes Servings: 6

Ingredients:
- 1 tbsp. coconut oil, melted
- 7 oz. cauliflower rice
- 4 oz. water
- 16 oz. coconut milk
- 3 oz. coconut sugar
- 1 egg
- 1 tsp. cinnamon powder
- 1 tsp. vanilla extract

Directions:
1. In a pan, combine the oil with the rice, water, milk, sugar, egg, cinnamon, and vanilla, whisk well, bring to a simmer, cook for 20 minutes over medium heat, divide into bowls and serve cold.
2. Enjoy!

Nutrition:

Calories: 78 Protein: 11 g
Carbs: 8 g Sodium: 51 mg
Fat: 1 g Potassium: 121.4mg

196. Coconut Mousse

Preparation time: 10 minutes Cooking time: 0 minutes Servings: 12

Ingredients:
- 2 and 3/4 cup coconut milk
- 1 teaspoon coconut extract
- 1 teaspoon vanilla extract
- 4 teaspoons coconut sugar

Dash Diet Cookbook

- 1 cup coconut, toasted

Directions:
1. In a bowl, combine the coconut milk with the coconut extract, vanilla extract, coconut and sugar, whisk well, set into small cups and serve cold. Enjoy!

Nutrition:
Calories: 359　　　　　　　　　Fat: 7 g　　　　　　　　　Protein: 14 g
Carbs: 6.1 g　　　　　　　　　Sodium: 19 mg　　　　　　Potassium: 132mg

197. Mango Pudding

Preparation time: 10 minutes　　　Cooking time: 50 minutes　　　Servings: 4

Ingredients:
- 1 cup brown rice
- 2 cups water
- 1 mango, peeled and chopped
- 1 cup coconut milk
- 2 tablespoons coconut sugar
- 1 teaspoon vanilla extract
- 1/2 teaspoon cinnamon powder

Directions:
1. Put the water in a pan and bring to a boil over medium heat.
2. Add rice, stir, cover the pan and cook for 40 minutes.
3. Add milk, sugar, vanilla, cinnamon and mango, stir, cover the pan again, cook for 10 minutes more, divide into bowls and serve.
4. Enjoy!

Nutrition:
Calories: 88　　　　　　　　　Fat: 9 g　　　　　　　　　Sodium: 74 mg
Carbs: 1 g　　　　　　　　　Protein: 1 g　　　　　　　Potassium: 167mg

198. Rhubarb Pie

Preparation time: 10 minutes　　　Cooking time: 25 minutes　　　Servings: 12

Ingredients:
- 2 cups whole wheat flour
- 1 cup low-fat butter, melted
- 1 cup pecans, chopped
- 1 and 1/4 cup coconut sugar
- 4 cups rhubarb, chopped
- 1 cup strawberries, sliced
- 8 ounces low-fat cream cheese

Directions:
1. In a bowl, combine the flour with the butter, pecans and 1/4 cup sugar and stir well.
2. Transfer this to a pie pan, press well into the pan, introduce in the oven and process at 350 degrees F for 20 minutes.
3. In a pan, combine the strawberries with the rhubarb, cream cheese and 1 cup sugar, stir well and cook over medium heat for 4 minutes.
4. Spread this over the pie crust and keep in the fridge for a few hours before slicing and serving.
5. Enjoy!

Nutrition:
Calories: 35　　　　　　　　　Fat: 2g　　　　　　　　　Sodium: 70 mg
Carbs: 5g　　　　　　　　　Protein: 0g　　　　　　　Potassium: 128mg

199. Fruit Skewers

Preparation time: 10 minutes Cooking time: 0 minutes Servings: 10

Ingredients:
- 5 strawberries, halved
- 1.4 cantaloupe, cubed
- 2 bananas, cut into chunks
- 1 apple, cored and cut into chunks

Directions:
1. Thread strawberry, cantaloupe, bananas and apple chunks alternately onto skewers and serve them cold.
2. Enjoy!

Nutrition:
Calories: 464   Carbs: 4.7g   Sodium: 52.1mg
Protein: 34.8g   Fat: 22.1g   Potassium: 198mg

200. Pumpkin Pudding

Preparation time: 1 hour Cooking time: 0 minutes Servings: 4

Ingredients:
- 1 and 1/2 cups almond milk
- 1/2 cup pumpkin puree
- 2 tbsp. coconut sugar
- 1/2 tsp. cinnamon powder
- 1/4 tsp. ginger, grated
- 1/4 cup chia seeds

Directions:
1. In a bowl, combine the milk with pumpkin, sugar, cinnamon, ginger, and chia seeds, toss well, divide into small cups and keep them in the fridge for 1 hour before serving.
2. Enjoy!

Nutrition:
Calories: 209   Carbohydrates: 2.2g   Sodium: 94.7mg
Fat: 6g   Protein: 17g   Potassium: 191.6mg

201. Pop Corn Bites

Preparation time: 5 minutes Cooking time: 2-3 minutes Servings: 4

Ingredients:
- 3 cups Medjool dates, chopped
- 12 ounces brewed coffee
- 1 cup pecan, chopped
- 1/2 cup coconut, shredded
- 1/2 cup cocoa powder

Directions:
1. Dip dates in warm coffee for 5 minutes. Detach dates from coffee and mash them, making a fine smooth mixture.
2. Set in remaining ingredients (except cocoa powder) and form small balls out of the mixture. Coat with cocoa powder, serve and enjoy!

Nutrition:
Calories: 376   Sodium: 76mg   Protein: 10g
Fat: 11g   Carbs: 6.7g   Potassium: 198mg

202. Delicious Berry Pie

Preparation time: 10 minutes Cooking time: 1 hour Servings: 6

Ingredients:
- 1/2 cup whole wheat flour
- Cooking spray
- 1/3 cup almond milk
- 1/4 tsp. baking powder
- 1/4 tsp. stevia
- 1/4 cup blueberries

- 1 tsp. olive oil
- 1 tsp. vanilla extract
- 1/2 tsp. lemon zest, grated

Directions:
1. In a bowl, mix flour with baking powder, stevia, blueberries, milk, oil, lemon zest, and vanilla extract, whisk, pour into your slow cooker lined with parchment paper and greased with the cooking spray, cover, and cook on High for 1 hour.
2. Leave the pie to cool down, slice, and serve.

Nutrition:
Calories: 92　　　　Fat: 4g　　　　Sodium: 55mg
Protein: 5g　　　　Carbs: 3g　　　　Potassium: 142mg

203. Gentle Sweet Potato Tempura

Preparation time: 10 minutes　　　Cooking time: 0 minutes　　　Servings: 4

Ingredients:
- 2 whole eggs
- 1/4 teaspoon salt
- 2 cups oil
- 3/4 cup ice water + 3 tablespoons ice water
- 1 sweet potato, scrubbed and sliced into 1/8-inch slices
- 3/4 cup all-purpose flour + 1 tablespoons all-purpose flour
- For sauce:
- 1/4 cup rice wine
- 1/4 cup coconut aminos

Directions:
1. Take a large bowl and beat in eggs until frothy.
2. Stir in salt, ice water, and flour, mix well until the batter is lumpy.
3. Take a frying pan and place over high heat, add oil and heat to 350°F.
4. Dry-sweet potato slices and dip 3 slices at a time in the batter, let excess batter drip Fry until golden brown on both sides, each side should take about 2 minutes.
5. Live them out and drain excess oil, keep repeating until all potatoes are done.
6. Take a small bowl and whisk in rice wine, soy sauce and use it as a dipping sauce. Enjoy!

Nutrition:
Calories: 269　　　　Fat: 9.7 g　　　　Sodium: 53 mg
Carbs: 1.7 g　　　　Protein: 25.6 g　　　　Potassium: 112.2mg

204. Delightful Pizza Dip

Preparation time: 20 minutes　　　Cooking time: 0 minutes　　　Servings: 10

Ingredients:
- 1 cup pureed ripe tomato
- 2 ounces shredded Colby cheese
- 8 ounces Ricotta cheese
- 1 teaspoon garlic paste
- 1/2 teaspoon dried basil
- 1/2 teaspoon dried oregano
- 1 teaspoon porcini powder
- 1 teaspoon shallot powder
- 1/4 teaspoon chipotle powder
- 1/2 cup Kalamata olives, to garnish
- 1/2 teaspoon crushed red pepper flakes
- 8 ounces chopped salami; a few slices reserved
- Flaky sea salt and ground black pepper

Directions:
1. Put your oven on at 360°F.
2. Merge all the ingredients together except for the olives and the reserved salami and put them in a casserole dish.
3. On the top put the extra salami slices and the olives and bake for 15 minutes.

4. Serve hot and enjoy!

Nutrition:
Calories: 70
Carbs: 1/5g
Fat: 0g
Protein: 2g
Sodium: 6 mg
Potassium: 192mg

205. Strawberry Cheesecake

Preparation time: 4 hours   Cooking time: 20 minutes   Servings: 8

Ingredients:
- 2 cups crumbled graham crackers;
- 7 tablespoons butter, melted;
- 16 oz. cream cheese, softened;
- 8 oz. whipped topping, thawed;
- 1 cup sour cream;
- 1 lb. fresh strawberries, halved;
- 3/4 cup sugar;
- 2 teaspoon vanilla extract.

Directions:
1. Mix crackers and butter in a bowl. Prepare a springform pan and coat with cooking spray.
2. Press the crust mixture into the bottom of the pan and refrigerate for 30 minutes. Set cream cheese and sugar in a bowl until smooth.
3. Add sour cream and vanilla, stir well to combine.
4. Fold in strawberries. Set the mixture on top of the crust and refrigerate for about 3-4 hours.

Nutrition:
Calories: 452
Fat: 22.3g
Carbs: 27.6g
Protein: 37.1g
Sodium: 13mg
Potassium: 191mg

206. Strawberries and Cream Cheese Crepes

Preparation time: 10 minutes   Cooking time: 10 minutes   Servings: 4

Ingredients:
- 4 tbsp. cream cheese, softened
- 2 tbsp. sifted powdered sugar
- 2 tsp. vanilla extract
- 2 prepackaged crepes, each about 8 inches
- 8 strawberries, hulled and sliced
- 1 tsp. powdered sugar for garnish
- 2 tbsp. caramel sauce, warmed

Directions
1. Heat the oven to 325F. Set the baking dish with cooking spray.
2. In a mixing bowl, merge the cream cheese until smooth using an electric mixer. Add the powdered sugar and vanilla. Mix well.
3. Set 1/2 of the cream cheese mixture on each crepe, leaving 1/2-inch around the edge. Top with 2 tbsp. of strawberries.
4. Roll up each crepe and place seam-side down in the prepared baking dish. Bake until lightly browned (about 10 minutes).
5. Cut the crepes in half. Transfer to four individual serving plates.

Nutrition:
Calories: 180
Fat: 5 g
Carbs: 1.9 g
Protein: 15 g
Sodium: 30 mg
Potassium: 178 mg

207. Apple-Berry Cobbler

Preparation time: 55 minutes   Cooking time: 40 minutes   Servings: 6

Ingredients:
The Filling:
- 1 cup fresh raspberries
- 1 cup fresh blueberries
- 2 cups chopped apples
- 2 tbsp. turbinado or brown sugar
- 1/2 tsp. ground cinnamon
- 1 tsp. lemon zest

- 2 tsp. lemon juice

The Topping:
- Egg white from 1 large egg
- 1/4 cup soy milk
- 1/4 tsp. salt
- 1 1/2 tbsp. cornstarch
- 1/2 tsp. vanilla
- 1 1/2 tbsp. turbinado or brown sugar
- 3/4 cup whole-wheat pastry flour

Directions:
1. Heat the oven to 350F. Lightly coat six individual ovenproof ramekins with cooking spray. 2. Attach the raspberries, blueberries, apples, sugar, cinnamon, lemon zest, and lemon juice in a medium bowl. Stir to mix evenly.
2. Attach the cornstarch and stir until it dissolves. Set aside.
3. In a separate bowl, attach the egg white and whisk until lightly beaten. Add the soy milk, salt, vanilla, sugar, and pastry flour. Stir to mix well.
4. Set the fruit mixture evenly among the prepared ramekins. Spill the topping over each. Place the ramekins on a large baking pan and place them in the oven.
5. Process until the filling is tender and the topping is golden brown (about 30 minutes).

Nutrition:
Calories: 252　　Carbs: 15 g　　Sodium: 15 mg
Fat: 7 g　　Protein: 12 g　　Potassium: 254 mg

208. Vanilla Poached Peaches

Preparation time: 10 minutes　　Cooking time: 30 minutes　　Servings: 4

Ingredients:
- 1 cup water
- 1/2 cup sugar
- 1 vanilla bean, split and scraped
- 4 large peaches, pitted and quartered
- Mint leaves or ground cinnamon, for garnish

Directions:
1. Set the water, sugar, vanilla bean into a saucepan. In a low heat, stir the mixture until the sugar dissolves. Continue to boil until the mixture thickens (about 10 minutes).
2. Attach the cut fruit. Low heat for about 5 minutes.

Nutrition:
Calories: 214　　Carbs: 7.7g　　Sodium: 16.6mg
Protein: 2.6g　　Fat: 19.8　　Potassium: 232mg

209. Mixed Berry Whole-Grain Cake

Preparation time: 15 minutes　　Cooking time: 35 minutes　　Servings: 8

Ingredients:
- 1/2 cup skim milk
- 1 tbsp. vinegar
- 2 tbsp. canola oil
- 1 tsp. vanilla
- 1 egg
- 1/3 cup packed brown sugar
- 1 cup whole-wheat pastry flour
- 1/2 tsp. baking soda
- 1/2 tsp. ground cinnamon
- 1/4 tsp. salt
- 1 cup frozen mixed berries, such as raspberries, blueberries and blackberries
- 1/4 cup low-fat granola, slightly crushed

Directions:
1. Heat the oven to 350F. Set the cake pan with cooking spray and coat with flour.
2. In a large bowl, merge the milk, vinegar, oil, vanilla, egg, and brown sugar until smooth.
3. Stir in the flour, cinnamon, baking soda and salt just until moistened.
4. Carefully fold half the berries into the batter.

5. Spoon the mixture into the prepared pan. Sprinkle with the remaining berries and top with the granola.
6. Process for 25 to 30 minutes or until golden brown and the top springs back when touched in the center.
7. Cool in the pan for 10 minutes.

Nutrition:

Calories: 329	Carbs: 1.4g	Sodium: 64mg
Fat: 14g	Protein: 17g	Potassium: 107mg

210. Ambrosia with Coconut and Toasted Almonds

Preparation time: 15 minutes Cooking time: 30 minutes Servings: 8

Ingredients:
- 1/2 cup slivered almonds
- 1/2 cup unsweetened shredded coconut
- 1 small pineapple, cubed
- 5 oranges, segmented
- 2 red apples, cored and sliced
- 1 banana, halved lengthwise, skinned, and sliced crosswise
- 2 tbsp. cream sherry
- Fresh mint leaves for garnish

Directions:
1. Heat the oven to 325F. Set the almonds on a baking sheet and bake, stirring occasionally, until golden and fragrant for about 10 minutes. Set immediately to a plate to cool.
2. Attach the coconut to the sheet and bake, stirring often, until lightly browned for about 10 minutes. Place immediately to a plate to cool.
3. In a large bowl, merge the pineapple, oranges, apples, banana, and sherry. Set gently to mix well.

Nutrition:

Calories: 359	Fat: 7 g	Protein: 14 g
Carbs: 6.1 g	Sodium: 19 mg	Potassium: 132mg

Chapter 9. Index

Acorn Squash with Apples 68
Almond and Tomato Balls 64
Almond Rice Pudding 89
Ambrosia with Coconut and Toasted Almonds 101
Antioxidant Smoothie Bowl 11; 13
Apple and Almond Muffins 92
Apple and Berry Cobbler 60
Apple Dumplings .95
Apple Oats 21
Apple Pie Crackers 42
Apple-Berry Cobbler 99
Apricot Biscotti 59
Aromatic Cauliflower Florets 67
Aromatic Whole Grain Spaghetti 82
Asian Style Asparagus 66
Asparagus with Horseradish Dip 68
Avo Trout Toastie 14
Avocado Tuna Bites 64
Baby minted carrots 83
Bacon Bits 17
Baked Falafel 83
Baked Smoky Broccoli and Garlic 78
Balsamic Roast Chicken Breast 49
Banana Custard 65
Banana-Cashew Cream Mousse 88
Basil Halibut 55
Bean Hummus 80
Black Bean Bake with Avocado 75
Black Bean Burgers with Lettuce "Buns" 31
Black Bean Stew with Cornbread 27
Black Eyed Peas and Spinach Platter 44
Black-Eyed Peas and Greens Power Salad 81
Braised Artichokes 69
Braised Baby Carrot 67
Breakfast Fruits Bowls 24
Broccoli Salad 77
Bruschetta Chicken 48
Brussel Sprouts Mix 67
Brussels sprouts with Shallots and Lemon 71
Buckwheat Crepes 21
Butternut-Squash Macaroni and Cheese 81
Caramelized Apricot Pots 91
Caramelized Blood Oranges with Ginger Cream 90
Carrot Cakes 82
Carrot Muffins 23
Cauliflower Bread Stick 61
Cauliflower Cinnamon Pudding 95
Cauliflower Lunch Salad 37
Cauliflower Salad with Tahini Vinaigrette 79
Cherry Stew 88
Chia Seeds Breakfast Mix 24
Chicken and Strawberry Salad 54
Chicken Caesar Pasta Salad 57
Chickpea Cauliflower Tikka Masala 39
Chickpea Curry 85
Chickpea Frittata with Tomatoes and Watercress 33
Chili-Lime Grilled Pineapple 71
Chocolate Avocado Mousse 92
Chunky Tomatoes 83
Cocktail Wieners .. 62
Coconut Mousse .. 95
Colorful Citrus Smoothie 14
Corn Stuffed Peppers 50
Cranberry Hot Wings 63
Creamy Pumpkin Pasta 26
Curry Tofu Scramble 22
Curry Vegetable Noodles with Chicken 32
Delicious Aloo Palak 56
Delicious Berry Pie 97
Delightful Pizza Dip 98
Easy Coconut-Carrot Cake Balls 94
Easy Lunch Salmon Steaks 36
Easy Veggie Muffins 22
Eggplant Bites with Marinara 76
Eggplant Parmesan Stacks 39
Everyday Vegetable Stock 43
Falafel with Mint-Tahini Sauce 75
Faux Mac and Cheese 65
Fig and Goat's Cheese Salad 52
Fish Stew 45
Flax Banana Yogurt Muffins 20
Fragrant Shakshuka 11; 13
French Toast Sticks with Yogurt-Berry Dipping Sauce 40
Fried Pasta Chips with Tomato-Basil Dip 73
Fruit Pizza 20
Fruit Skewers 97
Fruity Breakfast Muffins 16
Garden Salad 78
Garlic Black Eyed Peas 69
Generous Garlic Bread Stick 61
Gentle Sweet Potato Tempura 98
Glazed Eggplant Rings 85

Gnocchi Pomodoro 45
Gnocchi with Tomato Basil Sauce 26
Granola Parfait 22
Grilled Chicken with Lemon and Fennel 43
Grilled Eggplant Slices 70
Grilled Minted Watermelon 91
Grilled Tomatoes .68
Harissa Bolognese with Vegetable Noodles 33
Hassel back Eggplant 28
Hasselback Eggplant 80
Hasselback Eggplant Parmesan 57
Hazelnut-Parsley Roast Tilapia 52
Healthy Tahini Buns 66
Healthy Vegetable Fried Rice 81
Hearty Buttery Walnuts 64
Humble Mushroom Rice 44
Italian Stuffed Portobello Mushroom Burgers 40
Italian Style Zucchini Coins 70
Jack-o-Lantern Pancakes 20
Kale, Quinoa, and Avocado Salad 77
Key Lime Cherry "Nice" Cream 93
Leek and Cauliflower Soup 55
Leeks Soup 37
Lemon Cheesecake 92
Lemongrass and Chicken Soup 35
Lentil Sauté............70
Light Balsamic Salad 36
Loaded Potato Skins 86
Mango Pudding 96
Masala Chickpeas .53
Mexican-Style Potato Casserole 27
Mini Teriyaki Turkey Sandwiches 62
Mixed Berry Whole-Grain Cake 100
Mixed Fruit Compote Cups 60
Mixed Vegetable Salad with Lime Dressing 54
Mushroom Cakes .84
Mushroom Florentine 28
Mushroom Frittata 16
Mushroom Shallot Frittata 19
Mushrooms and Cheese Omelet 25
Mushrooms and Turkey Breakfast 25
No-Bake Breakfast Granola Bars 19
Orange and Chili Garlic Sauce 42
Orecchiette with Broccoli Rabe 53
Paella 84
Pan-Fried Salmon with Salad 30
Parsley Celery Root 69
Peach Crumble Muffins 63

Peanut Butter and Banana Breakfast Smoothie 18
Penne with Sizzling Tomatoes and Artichokes 74
Pineapple Oatmeal 23
Pop Corn Bites 97
Pressure Cooker Braised Pulled Ham 62
Pumpkin Cookies .24
Pumpkin Pie..........91
Pumpkin Pie Fat Bombs 59
Pumpkin Pudding 97
Purple Potato Soup 36
Quinoa Bowl.........86
Quinoa Power Salad 48
Quinoa-Lentil Burgers 76
Raspberry Polenta Waffles 15
Red Velvet Pancakes with Cream Cheese Topping 18
Refreshing Watermelon Sorbet 65
Rhubarb Pie 96
Roasted Apple–Butternut Squash Soup 34
Roasted Cauliflower and Lima Beans 79
Roasted Root Vegetables with Goat's Cheese Polenta 44
Roasted Salmon with Smoky Chickpeas and Greens...............47
Salmon Couscous Salad 46
Salmon with Salsa 47
Sautéed Bananas with Orange Sauce 90
Sautéed Swiss Chard 66
Slow-Cooked Pasta e Fagioli Soup 46
South Asian Baked salmon 51
Spicy Tofu Burrito Bowls with Cilantro Avocado Sauce 38
Spinach Ginger Lentils 55
Spinach Muffins ...23
Spinach, Mushroom, and Feta Cheese Scramble 18
Sriracha Parsnip Fries 88
Steel Cut Oat Blueberry Pancakes 17
Stone Fruit Quinoa 15
Strawberries and Cream Cheese Crepes 99
Strawberry Cheesecake 99
Stuffed Eggplant Shells 49
Sweet Almond and Coconut Fat Bombs 59
Sweet and Sour Cabbage and Apples 56
Sweet and Sour Vegetable Noodles 34
Sweet Potato and Bean Fry Up 17
Sweet Potato Balls 85
Sweet Potato Carbonara with Spinach and Mushrooms 51
Sweet Potatoes and Apples Mix 89

Sweet Potatoes and Zucchini Soup 35
Tantalizing Mushroom Gravy 42
Tart Raspberry Crumble Bar 94
Tempeh Veggie Tacos 32
Toasted Almond Ambrosia 93
Toasted Chickpea-Quinoa Bowl 73
Tofu and Green Bean Stir Fry 37
Tomato and Olive Orecchiette with Basil Pesto 40
Tortilla Strawberry Chips 89
Tuna Sandwich 35
Vanilla Poached Peaches 100
Veg Breakfast Taco 14
Vegan Chili 82

Vegan Meatloaf 86
Vegetable Noodles with Bolognese 31
Vegetable Pasta 30
Vegetarian Kebabs 29
Vegetarian Lasagna 29
Veggie Scramble ... 24
Veggie Variety 30
White Beans Stew 29
White Beans with Spinach and Pan-Roasted Tomatoes 80
Whole Grain Pancakes 21
Zucchini Fritters with Corn Salsa 72
Zucchini Lasagna Roll-Ups 72
Zucchini Pepper Kebabs 50

Chapter 10. BONUS: VIDEO LECTURES

The Dash diet can provide useful benefit for people suffering of HBP, reducing dependance on drugs. So, we thought that you would appreciate having 15 video lectures to consult to furtherly clarify some of the concepts discussed in this book.

You can find them at this link:

Video Lecture Link

Conclusion

Many people do not realize how much salt they consume in their regular diet. It is straightforward to go over your daily sodium allowance when eating at fast-food restaurants because the food often has a lot of salt. By eating at restaurants and not controlling your sodium intake, you could easily consume 3 or 4 times your daily salt limit. By switching to a dash diet, you can still go out to eat at restaurants and manage your salt consumption. The DASH diet will allow you to control your sodium consumption while allowing fast food at restaurants that may not have lower sodium choices.

The dash diet is a precise way to lose weight and lower blood pressure without spending hours cooking exotic recipes. This diet is also a great way to stay healthy. If you try to stick to the diet's prescribed foods, you can lose weight, lower your blood pressure, and lower your threat of heart disease. This diet is easy to follow and can be followed by anyone. It does not require a lot of time to shop for food or cook the food, making it easy for you to follow.

The dash diet is also very well suited to work with any lifestyle. If you have kids, you can ensure that they follow the proper portion sizes of the foods on the dash diet, so they will not overeat and gain weight. When you have high blood pressure, you must start eating right and reduce it. The dash diet is the precise way to do this. The dash diet does not demand you to be religious about what you eat, but it encourages heart-healthy foods such as fruits, vegetables, whole grains, and nuts. This cookbook is a way for you to lower your blood pressure quickly. By following these easy steps, you will reduce your blood pressure and increase the quality of your life.

If you enjoyed this book, we would really appreciate a review:
Review Link

Printed in Great Britain
by Amazon